BEYOND THE
LIMITS OF THE LAW

BEYOND THE
LIMITS OF THE LAW
CORPORATE CRIME
AND LAW AND ORDER

John L. McMullan

Fernwood Publishing, Halifax

Editing: Douglas Beall
Design and production: Beverley Rach
Printed and bound in Canada

Volume I of the *Crimes of Capital* Series

A publication of Fernwood Publishing

Fernwood Publishing, Box 9409 Station A
Halifax, Nova Scotia, B3K 5S3

First printing 1992
Second printing 1993

Canadian Cataloguing in Publication Data

McMullan, John L., 1948-

    Beyond the limits of the law

    Includes bibliographical references.
    ISBN 1-895686-03-2

1. Corporations -- Corrupt practices. 2. Commercial crimes. 3. Corporate profits -- Moral and ethical aspects. I. Title.

HV6768.M32 1992   364.1 68   C92-098581-5

Contents

Preface

This book is a crystallization of ideas that emerged from two settings. First, I am very indebted to the students at Saint Mary's University who participated in my critical criminology seminars between 1986 and 1991. What started off as no more than a set of questions and intuitions about crimes of the powerful led, through their interest and encouragement, to this volume on corporate crime. The other inspiration was my friendship with my colleague Bob Ratner. This book was originally conceived of as a chapter in a book to be written by Bob and me. While waiting for him to produce his chapters, I benefitted from his good humour and good sense and I also had enough time to write a longer treatise.

True to our original intentions, I wrote this book as a study in critical criminology. My basic purpose is to define, illustrate and analyze corporate crime. My approach, on the one hand, is to build my analysis around the relationship between economy, bureaucracy, law and the state, and corporate harm, homicide and exploitation and, on the other hand, to offer some radical remedies for the control and reduction of corporate crime.

Many students and colleagues helped along the way. I am especially indebted to the following people who took time away from their busy schedules to discuss, read and criticize the manuscript: Jo-Anne Fiske, Richard Hadden, Roberta Hamilton, Nanette Juliano, Ena MacDonald, Judy Mosoff, Bob Ratner, Jim Russell and John Whelan.

Special thanks go to Anne Creaser for preparing the manuscript, to Saint Mary's University for providing financial aid, to Douglas Beall for his careful editorial assistance and to Errol Sharpe for his interest and assistance in publishing the book.

• 1 •
Introduction

When people are asked to talk about crime, they often provide examples of offenses against persons, property and public order such as homicide, aggravated assault, larceny, illegal drugs, prostitution, or driving under the influence of alcohol. They tend to see and fear crime as something "out there" in the streets committed by desperate or deranged strangers. A common image is that of cool and defiant youth, scared and confused on the inside and resentful and fiercely independent on the outside. Cut off from the mainstream of industry, work and community, alone or in groups, they live in the street world of drugs, theft, interpersonal violence and prostitution.

There is nothing particularly wrong with this view. Such crimes do exist. Conventional crimes and the crimes of marginalized populations do need to be taken seriously. However, this is a partial and somewhat misleading understanding of what constitutes crime and where it occurs in society. Uniform crime reports and crime indices, though helpful in cataloguing certain forms of serious harm, rarely include the illegalities committed in corporate surroundings. "Thus we learn how many citizens were robbed or had their cars stolen each year, but we are not told how often corporations sold us defective automobiles or defrauded the public by fixing prices illegally. Even if only inadvertently, the statistical reports. . . send a distinct message: street crime, not white-collar or corporate lawlessness, is the real source of the crime problem" (Cullen, Maakestad and Cavender 1987, 41). Understanding the crime problem— its scope, harm and cost, and what can be done about it— means that we must look up, as well as down in the social order. Consider the following examples.

In May 1972, Mrs. Lilly Gray and 13-year-old Richard Grimshaw were driving in a Ford Pinto along a California highway when their car stalled. They were hit from behind by an automobile that had slowed down but could not avoid the collision. The Pinto immediately burst into flames. Mrs. Gray died shortly thereafter and Richard sustained burns to 90 percent of his body but lived. The Ford management knew of defects in the rear structure, the bumper, the rear wheels, the differential housing, the placement of the gas tank, the passenger doors, and the carburetor float. Crash tests prior to marketing had shown that the gas tank would rupture if hit from behind, even by cars moving at 21 miles per hour.

Corporate executives had full knowledge of these faults but deliberately decided not to correct them. They had calculated that they would save more than $85 million by delaying lifesaving correctives but would lose no more than $200,000 per death in legal suits. As a result, they chose to put profits before people. Here is how a company memorandum put it:

Benefits

Savings:	180 burn deaths, 180 serious burn injuries, 2,100 burned vehicles
Unit Cost:	$200,000 per death, $67,000 per injury, $700 per vehicle
Total Benefit:	(180 x $200,000) + (180 x $67,000) + (2,100 x $700) = $49.5 million

Costs

Sales:	11 million cars, 1.5 million light trucks
Unit Cost:	$11 per car, $11 per truck
Total Cost:	(11 million x $11) + (1.5 million x $11) = $137 million

This cold calculus suggested that delaying action on car improvement and safety was cost-effective and therefore desirable, even if such safety standards and correctives would result in fewer auto fires and fewer burn deaths and injuries (Dowie 1987b, 13-29; Kramer 1982, 75-94; Henry 1986, 184-186).

The asbestos industry has been linked to lung diseases since before World War I. Studies by academics and doctors and policy decisions by insurance companies and workers compensation boards have confirmed that asbestos dust has harmful effects on the respiratory system. People who inhale asbestos fibres may contract asbestosis, a lung disease similar to emphysema and/or several types of cancer (Swimmer and Luce 1985, 530). One study conducted by Dr. Irving Selikoff, found that the death rate of asbestos workers was well in excess of the average among all workers of the same age and sex. The deaths of 235 men in a sample of 632 asbestos workers were attributed to cancer or asbestosis — 174 more deaths than would normally be expected from these causes. The lung cancer rate was more than seven times normal.

The response of corporate executives in the industry has been to plead ignorance while at the same time withholding information regarding the dangers of asbestos, and to resist new government controls for health protection and to circumvent or ignore regulations that do exist. As one report on a Johns-Manville plant in Canada put it:

> As long as the man is not disabled, it is felt that he should not be told of his condition so that he can live and work in peace and the company can benefit by his many years of experience.

In that one asbestos mine, company doctors found that of 708 workers, only four (who had worked less than four years) had normal lungs (Sherrill 1987, 51). Over the past fifty years, thousands of painful and protracted deaths have resulted from illegal exposures to asbestos and from intentional cover-ups of its harmful and lethal effects. The deposition of Charles Roemer, a prominent attorney who worked for the Union Asbestos and Rubber Company, is informative. When Union Asbestos discovered that its workforce was being diseased by asbestos, it consulted with Johns-Manville officials to see if their physical examination program showed similar poor health results. According to Roemer, Manville's attorney replied, in effect:

> Sure, our x-rays show many of our workers have the disease, but we don't tell them they are sick because if we did, they would stop working and sue us . . . yes, we save a lot of money that way (Brodeur, 1985).

Approximately 11.5 million Americans, most of whom worked in asbestos plants and mines, suffer from asbestosis. Ten to eighteen percent of them, according to longitudinal studies, die from this lung disease. (Cullen, Maakestad and Cavender 1987, 69).

On the morning of February 15, 1982, the drilling unit *Ocean Ranger*, one of the world's largest semisubmersible rigs, capsized and sank on the

Grand Banks off Newfoundland, in the North Atlantic Ocean. The entire eighty-four-person crew was lost and the shock waves of this disaster reverberated through the local maritime communities and indeed throughout the world. Immediately after the sinking, the federal government of Canada, the provincial government of Newfoundland and other private American organizations set up and cooperated on inquiries to establish causes and seek prevention. Their reports are instructive.

The *Ocean Ranger*, it is safe to say, was primarily an instrument of profit. The pursuit of oil and gas reserves had developed in such a competitive and technological manner that "exploration on a worldwide scale [had moved] into deeper water under increasingly harsh environmental conditions" (Canada 1984, 111). Long-term human safety was increasingly put at risk for short-term speed in resource extraction.

The *Ocean Ranger* was built in Japan in 1976. It was designed to withstand 115-mile-an-hour winds and 100-foot seas and was expected to be able to withstand North Atlantic climactic conditions, including ocean storms and icebergs, although its classification did not guarantee seaworthiness or apply standards relating to "the thickness of portlights, or the protection of chain lockers from flooding" (ibid., 4, 7). The *Ocean Ranger* capsized after a loss of stability "caused by gravitation and the ingress of water into the forward ballast tanks and by flooding of the chain lockers and upper hull" of the rig, precipitated by severe winter storm conditions (ibid., 41). But the design of the rig also had the following flaws:

- it failed to specify portlights of adequate strength,
- it failed to provide a ballast control panel with components suitable for operation in a sea water environment,
- it possessed an unnecessarily complicated ballast control system and an inadequate electrical monitoring system that made the ballast control console susceptible to faults and information confusion, and
- it failed to provide a means to control water flooding into the chain lockers, and a permanently installed means of pumping out water (ibid., 139-42).

The command system on board the rig also was not geared to ensure safety. The drilling crew had priority over the marine crew. As the Royal Commission study (ibid., 37) noted, "the marine operations which assured the stability and safety of the rig were relegated to a subordinate role." The marine captain's role on the *Ocean Ranger* was secondary to the person in charge of oil drilling, who had "no marine qualifications, . . . no knowledge of the ballasting system or the principles of rig stability" but who ironically had the ultimate authority and responsibility for the safety of the rig and its crew. Even the ballast room operator "had no formal training in his functions or responsibilities." The rig was primarily a drilling platform for industrial exploitation and the marine presence on board ensured formal compliance, if nothing else, with regulatory rules. Indeed, the *Ocean Ranger* was operating in one of the most hazardous offshore environments in the world without any certificate of inspection of its seaworthiness - its last certification had expired fifty days before the sinking. It also had one of the worst safety records and a very lax and reactive system of regulation and safety enforcement (O'Neill 1987; House 1986).

Finally, there was little in the way of an evacuation plan for the rig, and "survival suits" were in short supply on board. As the Royal Commission observed, "these suits were commercially available at the time .... [and] had every man been properly protected by a survival suit, there is a real probability that some of them would have survived" (Canada, 1984, 140). Nor were emergency reserve operations effective or well coordinated. The response time was slow and confused, key personnel were not properly trained in rescue and medical procedures, and standby helicopters and ships were not provided with basic rescue equipment such as hoists, cranes, and rescue baskets and nets (ibid., 140, 150-52). Former *Ocean Ranger* Captain Karl Nehring, aptly summed up the corporate priorities: "The most important thing . . . [for them] is to keep the bit turning. Keep the drill turning. Never mind the safety of the people. Never mind if they get injured. Keep it turning" (quoted in O'Neill 1987, 161).

The oil rig was truly an instrument of immediate gain, not long-term worker safety. Tragically, it highlights the fact that victims of corporate negligence and harm in the workplace are many, and the violence of corporations has rightfully been called "corporate homicide" (Brodeur 1985, Epstein 1979, 81-86, 93; Henry 1986, 197-99; Hills 1987; Snider 1988, 236; Swartz 1978, 115-18).

Or consider the case of the last frontier, space. On the bitterly cold morning of January 28, 1986, the NASA space shuttle, *Challenger*, disintegrated minutes after liftoff. A presidential inquiry revealed a tangled web of NASA mismanagement, fraud and corporate misconduct:

- Engineers warned that the solid booster rocket might be defective at low outdoor temperatures.
- Top management, nevertheless, overruled their own engineers and gave approval for the flight. Strong pressure from

the senior-level executives at Morton Thiokol and from NASA officials to obtain a lucrative $400-million solid booster contract lay behind the decision to overrule the engineers and launch the craft.
- As early as 1980, safety issues were being suppressed: Rockwell International, the prime contractor for the space shuttle, failed to report promptly equipment and component defects on the space orbiter, and Jet Air Inc., a subcontractor for Rockwell, routinely falsified x-ray reports to hide defective welds on the space craft. Both defects were threatening to the *Challenger* and its crew (Hills 1987, 192-93).

Seven astronauts died in this "high tech homicide," their bodies vapourized in a fiery ball that lit up the sky and the television screens of millions and millions of viewers worldwide.

Physically disabling toxic substances are much in the news these days. From the famous "Love Canal" incident of the 1960s to the chemical waste spills in Ontario and Quebec in the late 1980s, it had become popularly known that PCBs, arsenic, mercury, lead, industrial wastes, gaseous fluorides and other chemicals are dangerous to health and environment (Tallmer 1987, 111-20). Perhaps the best known case of toxic waste violation in Canada is that of the Reed Paper Company, located in northwestern Ontario. Between 1960 and 1972, the company released 9,000 kilograms of mercury into the nearby river and lake system, polluting the river to a level double that considered safe. Certain fish species were found to have average mercury concentrations of 7.8 parts per million, almost sixteen times the government-defined "safe level" of 0.5 parts per million.

Despite requests, and a ban ordered by the federal government in 1970, the Reed Paper Company continued to discharge toxic chemicals into the river and lake system, to such a degree that it is estimated the water system will remain contaminated for at least another fifty years. This has ruined the traditional fishing economy of local Native communities and led to serious long-term health problems for those who ingested the mercury through eating of contaminated fish. This chemical poison has been found to cause deafness, muteness and blindness and to destroy brain tissue. The mercury pollution was finally halted in 1975, when the corporation changed its production technology (Castrilli 1982, 332-401; Goff and Reasons 1986, 220; Shkilnyk 1985, 187-91). But that was too little too late. By 1979, Kai Erikson (1985, xiii) observed that Grassy Narrows, one of the Native communities affected, was in his words "more deeply damaged than any community I had ever seen. Or heard about. Or even imagined."

In 1971, the Dalkon Shield, a contraceptive intrauterine device (IUD) was marketed in North America. After a few months of introduction, women began to complain of complications arising from its use, which included severe infections, blood poisoning, tubal pregnancies, spontaneous abortions, and abrasions and punctures of the uterine wall. By 1974 the Dalkon Shield had killed seventeen women and infected and injured another 200,000. According to one consultant, approximately 87,000 of the estimated 2.2 million American women who used the IUD suffered physical harm and chronic pain. Worldwide the death toll is unknown but suspected to be in "the hundreds—possibly thousands—of women" (Mintz 1985, 3-4).

But the Shield initially was not removed from the marketplace. Instead, corporate executives of A.H. Robins dumped their product onto foreign, Third World markets. Several million unsterilized units in bulk packages were distributed through the U.S. Agency for International Development's Office of Population. Profits were plentiful. A.H. Robins sold more than 4.5 million Dalkon Shields worldwide for $4.35 each, a good price for a device that cost only 25 cents to produce (Sherrill 1987, 51). The risk to these women was justified by the argument that any contraceptive device was better than none, especially since birth rates were so high in Third World countries.

Robins' corporate executives had knowingly promoted global distribution of a product it knew posed a serious health threat to women. By 1985, more than 14,000 victims had filed civil suits or non-litigated claims for compensation, and juries had awarded almost $25 million in punitive damages (Mintz 1987, 30-40). The Dalkon Shield case is not an isolated incident of corporate lawlessness. According to Mintz (1985, 247), who studied this case in detail:

> Yes, Robins — knowingly and willfully — put corporate greed before human welfare, suppressed scientific studies that would ascertain safety and effectiveness, concealed hazards from consumers, the medical profession and government, assigned a lower value to foreign lives than to American lives, behaved ruthlessly toward victims who sued, and hired outside experts who would give accommodating testimony. Yet almost every other major drug company has done one or more of these things, and some have done them repeatedly or routinely, and continue to do so. Some have been criminally prosecuted and convicted, and are recidivists.

By the time the U.S. government got around to investigating the Dalkon Shield, most of the product had been sold. Eventually it was removed from the marketplace (Mintz 1987, 30-40).

Between 1958 and 1978, Canadians were put out of pocket by $12 billion because of overcharging by the major oil companies. The report entitled *The State of Competition in the Canadian Petroleum Industry* (Canada 1981) documents the utter lack of competition in the industry and exposes price-fixing at every stage: the importation of pipelines, refining, marketing and distribution. The study shows that the intent of the four major companies — Imperial, Shell, Texaco, and Gulf — was to use Canada as a laboratory for price-fixing techniques. The report found "a deliberate tendency of the major companies to follow parallel action out of tacit recognition of their mutual self-interest."

Raids on oil companies and 200,000 pages of seized documents point clearly to the conclusion that the corporate giants conspired to manipulate prices. Their purpose was to reduce, if not eliminate, independent petroleum dealers. The best example was their common strategy to sell large volumes of gasoline at discount prices in order to force independent dealers out of business. According to the report, the large companies were successful because by 1978 most surviving independents "have faithfully followed the price structure established by the majors," and because between 1968 and 1978 the independents' share of the gas market was cut in half. By 1981 they held less than 15 percent of the Canadian market. Furthermore, the loss to consumers of $12 billion has not been recovered, although the result of price-fixing and overcharging has been higher profit for the major oil corporations (Anderson 1981, 36-40; Canada 1981).

Finally, bribery, corruption, kickbacks and influence-peddling have existed in many Western democratic states. Four recent revelations in Canada are instructive about corporate criminality. In June 1979, five prominent Canadian businessmen were convicted and sentenced to from two to five years in prison for defrauding public institutions by conspiring and fixing bids on harbour dredging contracts. In November 1983 the Amway Corporation and Amway of Canada Ltd. were found guilty of cheating the Federal state of more than $28 million in unpaid import duties between 1965 and 1980 (Goff and Reasons 1986, 209-10). The Montreal Olympics of 1976 and Calgary Olympics of 1986 were marred by several illegal transactions, including the offering of benefits and bribes by contractors for business preferences, excessive cost overruns, attempts to influence the bidding process, favouritism curried through gift-giving, and undeclared conflicts of interest (Auf der Maur 1976;

Reasons 1984). Indeed, in 1983 the former chairman of Montreal's municipal executive committee was fined $75,000 and jailed for one day for accepting a luxury house from an engineering firm that had received $7.2 million in contracts for Olympic stadium construction work (Reason 1984).

In 1991, sixteen prominent Canadian politicians, political aides, senior administrators, civil servants and law enforcers were charged with conspiracy to commit fraud or obstruct justice in connection with an alleged kickback and bribery scam. The allegations were pursued by a Quebec businessman, Glen Kealey, who claimed that some of the most powerful figures in the Conservative Party of Canada conspired illegally to defraud the federal government "by bribery, bid-rigging, kickbacks, falsehood or other fraudulent means." This is "Canada's Watergate," says Mr. Kealey, who in a private prosecution also alleged that a network of Conservative politicians and developers collected 5-10 percent of the value of business contracts awarded by the federal government. Hundreds of millions of dollars worth of contracts were said to be defrauded by the bid-fixing, kickbacks and bribes. The charges were laid after seventeen days of testimony from RCMP officers, cabinet ministers, members of parliament and political aides.

Michel Gravel, a former conservative MP, already has been convicted on fifteen counts of fraud and influence peddling and sentenced to one year in jail and fined $50,000 for his part in this tangled web of corporate crime and political corruption. According to Gravel, he was not alone and he now has implicated senior party politicians and advisors in the organized fraud. He claims that the small-fry backbench MPs have taken the rap while the big fish have escaped. As he puts it, "everyone is always pointing the finger at me, . . . okay, I collected the money, but I didn't keep the money." Both Gravel and Kealey's allegations point to a criminal conspiracy of large magnitude. The case was before the courts as this book was being written (*Globe and Mail*, June 22, July 18-20, 1991).

All these examples afford us a different image of the crime problem. Crimes of the powerful are not only harmful and dangerous acts, they also are common and costly. They are committed not by an underclass of the dispossessed and demoralized but by an upperclass of well heeled business officials with conventional values and respectable identities (Snider 1988, 238). Their crimes are enacted in suites, not on the streets, and they seem to be a persistent part of boardroom decision-making.

Clinard and Yeager (1980, 116-18), in their study of publicly owned manufacturing corporations in the United States, found that in two years alone "approximately three-fifths of the [477] . . . . corporations had at least one action initiated against them" and one-quarter of the firms "had multiple cases of non-minor violations." A more recent study of violations of antitrust laws involving *Fortune* 500 companies found that almost all companies had at least one violation, and that "the mean for those firms which were involved in . . . . illegal activity was three acts" (Kesner, Victor and Lamont 1986, 794). A study in 1985 concluded that "one out of every seven companies producing toxic wastes may have dumped illegally in recent years," polluting the environment unnecessarily (Cullen, Maakestad and Cavender 1987, 78). So endemic is corporate crime to the economy that it is difficult to explain it away as an oddity or exception. Is it really the case that the corporate executives at Ford, Johns-Manville, Reed Paper, Amway, Shell, Imperial, Texaco, Gulf, NASA and A.H. Robins acted out of failure or because they were 'socialized' into corporate misconduct and crime?

Many studies, particularly those of a liberal or conservative bent, try to explain corporate violations in terms of differential criminal socialization and individual motivation. They say that individuals learn criminal behaviours in the corporation because they associate in a subculture of immorality (Clinard 1979; Lane 1977; Geis 1978). As Sutherland, in an early empirical study of corporate crime, observed, "a person in an appropriate situation engages in such (corporate) criminal behaviour if, and only if, the weight of the favourable definitions exceeds the weight of the unfavourable definitions" (1961, 234). Other studies have tried to isolate personal psychological factors related to corporate crime, stressing aggressive personalities, moral development, moral conduct, and propensity for violence (Blum 1972; Monahan and Novaco 1979). The emphasis has been for the most part on individuals and their needs, goals, attitudes and behaviours, and on describing how and explaining why persons in positions of trust violate the law (Lane 1977).

I want to develop a different perspective. Corporate crime, as my examples show, is *organizational crime,* and understanding it requires that we get to the root of what I believe produces and reproduces it — to the workings of the economy, the corporate bureaucracy, the law and the state. In Chapter 2, I define my terms of reference and illustrate the scope of the corporate crime problem — the amount of violence, the harms and injuries, and the economic and social costs. I develop a typology of corporate crime. In Chapter 3, I offer an understanding of corporate crime. I focus on the dynamic of capital accumulation and on the corporate organizational context and stress the role of profits, product goals, gender and corporate rules, structures and beliefs in creating corporate theft, harm and homicide. In Chapter 4, I ask: What stands in the way of corporate crime? What is the role of the law and the state in remedying the potential for corporate abuse and crime? What legal liability exists through detection, enforcement, penalty and social censure? Finally, in Chapter 5, I propose some radical solutions for law and order in the corporate suites and in Chapter 6, conclude by examining the importance of a social movement against corporate crime.

• 2 •
The Corporate Crime Problem

It is essential at the outset to define as precisely as possible the nature of corporate crime. Clearly, like many crimes of capital, corporate crime is a business racket that champions the triumph of money over morality (Conklin 1977), but it needs more careful formulation if it is not to be confused with other crimes which share some of the same characteristics. Michalowski (1985, 314) suggests the following broad definition of crimes of capital:

> Crimes of capital are socially injurious acts that arise from the ownership or management of capital or from occupancy of positions of trust in institutions designed to facilitate the accumulation of capital.

Thus, white-collar occupational crime, corporate crime, organized crime and certain types of political crime qualify as crimes of capital.

Although Michalowski is right to concentrate on the economic dimension of crimes of capital, it is important to note that there are distinctions to be made among illegal pursuits of economic gain. For instance, corporate crime is clearly committed *for* the corporation and not against it. As Cullen, Maakestad and Cavender (1987, 40) remark, "the crucial point . . . is that the individuals involved in corporate criminality are acting on behalf of the organization and not primarily for direct personal gain — although higher corporate profits, including these obtained illegally, may bring executives such personal benefits as promotions, bonuses and salary increases."

Thus, crimes such as employee embezzlement, fraud and white-

collar employee theft are important crimes of capital, but they will not be
included in our discussion of corporate crime. Similarly, some political
crimes may be directly related to the advancement of financial goals and
capital growth. Thus accepting or offering bribes, legislative favouritism,
manipulating campaign contributions for economic or political gains,
violating civil rights, influence peddling, agent provocateurism and
"dirty tricks" political campaigning are all crimes of the state where state
officials and political officeholders utilize their power in illegal and
socially injurious ways to ingratiate themselves with private capital.
Interesting and important as these activities are, they nevertheless stand
for the most part outside our examination of corporate crime.

For our purposes, corporate crime will be defined following Schrager
and Short (1978, 409) and Box (1983, 20-22) as:

> illegal acts of omission or commission of an individual or group
> of individuals in a legitimate formal organization in accordance
> with the operative goals of the organization which have a serious
> physical or economic impact on employees, consumers, the
> general public and other organizations.

What this definition implies should be made clear. First, it does not
say that there must be intention for corporate crime to exist. Indifference
may very well be the greater cause of avoidable human harm, and so
corporate crime is conceptualized to include acts of omission as well as
obvious and purposive acts of commission (Box 1983, 31; Hills 1987, 187-
206; Reiman 1979, 61). Second, corporate crime is necessarily organizational crime, and the pursuit of organizational objectives is deeply
involved among the causes of corporate crime. As Kramer (1982, 80)
notes, "the goals of the organization, the structure of the organization,
[and] the environment of the organization have a significant relationship
to corporate criminal behaviour." This means that the behaviour of
individuals in corporations must be viewed within the structure of
bureaucracy and its organizational way of life (Vaughan 1983, 67-87).
Third, the victims of corporate crime may be harmed physically as well
as economically, and they include other corporations and nation-states in
addition to employees, consumers and the public (Goff and Reasons
1986, 204-5; Hills 1987; Vaughan 1979). Lastly, the focus on "illegal acts
and socially injurious acts" means that corporate crime is not limited to
acts specifically prohibited under criminal law. It also includes acts
prohibited under civil, regulatory and administrative law and even some
acts not presently under the control of law, such as analogous forms of
social injury that are violations of fundamental civil and human rights

(Michalowski 1985, 314-18; Schwendinger and Schwendinger 1970, 143; Box 1983, 22).

In addition to crimes for corporations (which benefit both the organizations and the individuals) and crimes against corporations (which benefit only the individual and victimize the organization), there are also criminal syndicates or criminal organizations. These are "structurally coordinated and bureaucratically organized associations of individuals" that are deliberately established, co-opted or managed for the "explicit purpose of executing criminal activity" (Michalowski 1985, 368; Box 1983, 22; O'Malley,1987, 80). Both criminal organizations and legitimate corporations break the law as a means of accumulating capital, but the difference is that the stated goals of legitimate business organizations are legal while those of criminal corporations are decidedly illegal. Furthermore, lawbreaking is an auxiliary process to aid goal achievement in legitimate enterprises, but for criminal organizations it is a central feature. Examples of this are provided by Croft (1975), Levi (1981, 1984) and Francis (1988) in their work on long-term fraud. They show how companies were created with the explicit intention of using them to obtain products on credit for which payment was never intended to be made, and thus the sole raison d'être of the enterprises was to carry out explicitly criminal projects.

Crimes of criminal corporations and corporate crime are two varieties of crimes of capital. They each have specific connections with accumulating or facilitating the accumulation of capital. O'Malley (1987, 80) notes:

> It can be recognized that capital which operates in prohibited fields must organize production and circulation of commodities in a fashion which differentiates it from capital working in the legitimate sector.

In this book I will concentrate on capital that operates in legitimate fields. Thus the activities of so called black market enterprises in drugs, gambling, prostitution, extortion, racketeering, labour corruption, arms smuggling and the like will not be examined, despite their intrinsic interest and importance to the overall accumulation of capital. The topic of organized crime and its relationship to legitimate capital is complex and deserving of a separate study.

The prevalence of corporate crime is well documented. Corporate crime is violent. Corporate crime injures. Corporate crime robs (Box 1983; Ellis 1986; Clinard and Yeager 1980; Snider 1988; Hills 1987). The physically harmful effects of corporate crime are difficult to assess precisely. In the United States, avoidable industrial diseases, accidents and deaths occur much more frequently than the crime of homicide. As Reiman (1979, 68) points out, "in the time it takes for one murder on the crime clock (one every twenty-six minutes), six workers have died 'just trying to make a living'!" Similarly, in the United Kingdom, the combined number of workers who died from fatal accidents and occupational diseases for the years 1973 to 1979 far exceeded the number of police-reported homicide cases. A conservative estimate puts the ratio at approximately seven to one (Box 1983, 28).

An equally disturbing picture emerges when we consider the relevant information for Canada. As the Law Reform Commission (1986, 5) notes: "In 1982, there were 854 fatal on-the-job accidents in Canada, and more than half a million cases of disabling accidents or work-related illnesses. Between 1972 and 1981, more than 10,000 Canadians died from injuries received on the job." In the Canadian province of Ontario alone in 1983, $943 million dollars in claims was paid out to injured and incapacitated workers. (Wente 1984, 46). The risks of work deaths are highest in the primary industries, especially forestry, mining and fishing. Nationally, the fatality rate in forestry in 1982 was 119.7 deaths per 100,000 employees and in mining it was 83.6 (ibid.). One Canadian worker dies on the job every two hours, and one injury occurs every six seconds (Reasons, Ross and Paterson 1981; Reasons 1987, 7).

According to Ellis (1986, 94-95), in Canada "the corporate death rate is more than six times greater" than the lethal street crime rate for murder and manslaughter. If official statistics on work-related injuries are compared with statistics on criminal code assaults in Canada, then the corporate assault rate is conservatively estimated to be twenty-five times greater than the conventional street assault rate. Furthermore, if death and injuries are considered together as a measure of total violent crime, then the "corporate rate of violence is twenty-eight times greater than the violent street crime rate" (ibid., 95).

But even these ratios put the best possible light on avoidable death in the workplace. We can be fairly sure that the recorded homicide rates are reasonably reliable, but we cannot have the same trust in the data on occupationally related deaths. As Snider (1988, 236-37) observes:

> The corporate sector and its allies . . . argue vociferously that such acts are purely accidental, and therefore, not crimes. Thus, victims often do not know anyone to whom they can report their injuries. Sometimes they do not even know the cause of their victimization — companies have denied that working conditions, additives or toxic discharges are unsafe or do any harm to

the health or safety of their employees or the public. . . . Faced
with the massive economic and political power of corporations
which favour non-enforcement; understaffed and often underfunded regulatory bodies frequently lacking the support of the
government that appointed them; confronting the high cost of
investigating . . . all this, then, makes it very difficult to ascertain
just how many corporate crimes are "really" occurring.

The ambiguity and even manipulation regarding the cause of death, the
reluctance and caution of enforcement agencies, and the general reti-
cence of corporations combine to depress levels of recorded industrial
death and injury below the level it would otherwise be. Nevertheless, in
Canada, occupational deaths were the third leading cause of death after
heart disease and cancer, and about 50 percent of these deaths are
attributable to unsafe and often illegal working conditions (Reason, Ross,
Paterson 1981).

The Law Reform Commission (1986) estimates that 135,000 employees in Ontario are directly or indirectly exposed to at least ten different
varieties of hazardous workplace pollutants, and Casey (1985) reports
that 250,000 to 500,000 workers nationwide are needlessly exposed to
radioactive and chemical pollutants each year.

In the United Kingdom more than 600 people die in work-related
accidents every year, and another 18,000 suffer major injuries from work-
related incidents. About 750 people die each year from occupational
diseases and the Health and Safety Executive and its inspectorates have
stated repeatedly that at least two out of three deaths and countless
injuries are preventable. Management has been cited as responsible for
three of every five farm deaths, two of every three deaths in general
manufacturing, 78 percent of fatal maintenance accidents in manufacturing and 70 percent of construction industry deaths (Pearce and Tombs
1990, 426).

In the USA, 14,000 people are killed in industrial "accidents" each
year and data from the study of one state indicates that 45 percent of all
industrial accidents result from violations of safety regulations. About
100,000 persons in the USA die annually from diseases caused by the
work they do; 390,000 workers are disabled on the job; and regulatory
inspectors regularly find lawbreaking in 75 percent of the firms they
investigate (Coleman 1989, 6; Simon and Eitzen 1986). All this contrasts
with 20,000 murders per year in a country with one of the highest
homicide rates in the industrial world. In Canada, in 1981 the officially
reported numbers of corporate assaults and deaths was 1,210,000 and
960, respectively, whereas the criminal code assault and death figures

were 112,911 and 648 (Ellis 1986, 94-95). Nor do statistics tell the whole story. Numbers, as Brodeur (1985) notes, "are human beings with the tears wiped off". They do not capture the agony of occupationally related homicide.

Consider the case of Stefan Golab, a 61-year-old Polish immigrant working for Film Recovery Systems, a Chicago-based recycling firm that extracted silver from film negatives by dipping them in a cyanide solution. The day after Christmas 1982, Film Recovery Systems hired Golab to clean the vats containing the cyanide solution. On February 16, 1983, Golab collapsed in the plant, shaking violently and foaming at the mouth; he then lapsed into unconsciousness and died before reaching a hospital. An autopsy showed that the cause of death was poisoning by cyanide fumes. Subsequent investigation and prosecution revealed that corporate officials:

> had ignored repeated instances of workers becoming nauseous and vomiting; had hired mostly illegal aliens who could not speak English and had failed to warn them of the dangers of cyanide; had clearly violated safety regulations by equipping employees with only paper facemasks and cloth gloves before assigning them to work on open vats containing cyanide; had scraped skull-and-crossbones warnings off drums of cyanide; and had such inadequate ventilation that the plant's air was a thick yellow haze with a distinct cyanide odor, which exceeded safety standards by containing four times the accepted level of cyanide (Cullen, Maakestad and Cavender 1987, 70-71).

After a two-month trial, Film Recovery System officials were convicted of three counts of murder and fourteen counts of reckless conduct. Three executives were sentenced to twenty-five years in prison and fined $10,000 each. The Company was fined $24,000. In rendering his decision, Judge Banks observed that so much corporate crime is planned at a distance from the harm it causes. "This is not a case of taking a gun and shooting someone. It is more like leaving a time bomb in an airport and then running away. The bomb kept ticking . . . until Stefan Golab died" (ibid., 1987, 71).

Mining catastrophes are often the site of agonizing deaths. The 1976 disaster in Kentucky in which twenty-six people died is but one example. It began when the mine's ventilation system malfunctioned and allowed dangerous quantities of explosive methane gas to drift into a shaft 2,000 feet below the surface. Supervisors failed to monitor the gas leak in accordance with safety guidelines and unsuspecting workers entered the area filled with methane. They died in a ball of flame when sparks from machinery ignited the gas. Before the explosion the mining corporation had been cited for 652 safety violations, including 60 for inadequate ventilation. Nor did a sense of outraged justice follow the carelessness, illegality and official neglect of the company. It received five hundred new citations for safety infractions in the thirteen months that followed the disaster (Reiman 1979, 45-46).

Springhill, Nova Scotia, 1958, is a place and date etched in the memories of many Canadians. On October 23 at 8:06 p.m. the ground shook and a booming explosion was heard. Over the next two weeks, 174 people were removed from the No. 2 mine — 74 of them were dead. It began when a "bump" in the mine suddenly let go. The coal face collapsed, burying the miners alive. One hundred miners were rescued: eighty-one men by October 29th, eleven more on October 30th and the remaining eight survivors on November 1st. But this was not the first time Springhill miners had been "caught in a bump." Between 1917 and 1958, 525 bumps in the No. 2 mine had claimed fourteen lives. Four years earlier, a severe bump brought about by the company's policy of lining up underground wall faces had killed five miners. Next an explosion caused by a dangerously located power cable and unsafe and illegal amounts of methane in the mine's atmosphere further eroded miners' confidence in company practices and policy. Then a bump in March 1958, precipitated by aligning the mine's walls, had killed one more miner. It was the beginning of the end (McKay 1987).

Bumps are common in deep mines such as the No. 2. When they occur, the coal seam and/or the rock strata associated with it suddenly shatter. The coal face is often expelled into the open areas of the mine, and sometimes the floor heaves and timber and roof splinter and collapse. This is roughly what occurred in 1958. But bumps are not natural; they are manmade. The disaster of 1958 was foreseen by rank-and-file miners and by the community. However, their concerns and protests over mine safety and the methods of mining were ignored. McKay (1987, 177-78) notes:

> The miners' worry that the company was making things worse by aligning the walls was apparently justified . . . . the company acted as any efficient corporate enterprise. . . . preferring the advice of its own engineers to the opinion of its workers . . . . the disaster offers us a modern case of the way expert knowledge can mislead, and how the decline of workers' control in production can harm an entire community. The blame rests . . . on the entire system which made it impossible to place a moratorium on

mining in No. 2, without destroying the local economy, until the phenomenon of bumping was better understood.

The aftermath to the disaster was not kind to the community of Springhill. The Royal Commission called to investigate the causes of the crisis absolved the company of any responsibility. Dominion Coal Company promptly decided not to reopen the mines and the exodus from the community had a considerable impact. The company escaped from Springhill unscathed, without even offering an apology. The community that remains and remembers still mourns its many losses and suffers the injustice alone.

Working women and men face constant danger in industrial settings as well as in office, clerical and service settings. Food processing plants may be hazardous to health. They require employees to slash, cut, crop and chop in quick succession while using sharp knives or saws. Injuries in the form of cuts, loss of fingers, burns and scalds are not uncommon; nor is job stress (Armstrong and Armstrong 1983, 128) At one poultry processing plant, chickens are moved along a conveyor belt at the rate of fifty-eight per minute, or 3,480 birds an hour. Meat cutters make eighty-seven separate body movements each minute, or 5,220 movements an hour. The pace of the line, combined with the physical requirements of the job, contributes to mental fatigue, ulcers and repetitive strain injuries (DeKeseredy and Hinch 1991,103).

Nor is office and clerical work free from preventable danger and harm. Poor lighting, poor ventilation, hazardous chemicals in the office, prolonged sitting, noise, and radiation from video display terminals put women and men at risk and create health problems, including stress, ulcers, hypertension, pneumonitis, eye, nose and throat irritations, back injuries, circulation problems, birth defects, cancers and sterility (Armstrong and Armstrong 1983; Reason, Ross and Paterson 1981; Chenier 1982). Telephone operators, for example, frequently suffer from tendonitis and carpal tunnel syndrome caused by repeated rapid hand and wrist movements that produce swelling and nervous disorders in the wrists and shoulders. One operator described it as follows:

> Last week I was not getting out very many calls. . . . I have a sort of chronic arthritis or something in the right shoulder and my arm felt as heavy as lead that day (quoted in Armstrong and Armstrong 1983, 134).

Bars, banks, convenience stores and gas stations can also be work settings hazardous to health. Sexual harrassment and assault, robbery, violent abuse and murder are stark realities, especially for women, in the service sector. One woman describes her experience as a waitress:

> I've had one night where a bullet went between my legs. In another nightclub . . . a guy grabbed me by the throat — he was actually choking me (ibid., 188).

But even these illustrations, comparisons and figures understate the extent of corporate-induced death and harm because they do not include reference to consumers physically injured by unsafe products or environmental pollution. As Box (1983, 27) writes:

> Don't feel safe staying home! The long arm of the corporations grim reaper is not deterred by such agoraphobic precautions. Consumers may be poisoned in their beds by improperly tested medical drugs, they may be killed over their dinner tables by unhygienically prepared food, they may be blown up to God knows where by the neighborhood chemical complex exploding, and they may become fatally diseased in their living rooms by industrial pollution.

Indeed, the U.S. Product Safety Commission estimates that 20 million serious injuries and 30,000 deaths result annually from hazardous goods and products being sold in the marketplace (Coleman 1989, 6). One of its studies discovered that 147 out of 847 fabrics failed to meet flammability standards, eight out of fifteen models of baby cribs were defective, 753 out of 1,338 toys were dangerous and 117 out of 148 products were unsafely packaged (Schrager and Short 1978, 415). The meat packing industry was found to be contaminated. Thirty-five of 65 poultry operations inspected by the U.S. General Accounting Office were seriously contaminated, while 18 of 216 and 31 of 57 meat packing plants in North Dakota and Massachusetts, respectively, were characterized by unsanitary conditions. Simon and Eitzen (1986, 102), in their study of elite deviance, provide the following related example:

> In 1984, Nebraska Beef Processors and its Colorado subsidiary, Cattle King Packing Company — the largest supplier of ground meat to school lunch programs and also a major supplier of meat to the Defense Department, supermarkets and fast-food chains — was found guilty of: (1) regularly bringing dead animals into its slaughter houses and mixing rotten meat into its hamburgers; (2) labeling old meat with phony dates; and (3) deceiving U.S.

Department of Agriculture inspectors by matching diseased carcasses with the healthy herds from larger cows. . . . In 1979, a New Jersey firm was convicted of making pork sausage with an unauthorized chemical which masks discoloration of spoiled meat. And in 1982, a California company used walkie-talkies to avoid inspectors while doctoring rotten sausage.

Corporate culpability is also high in the marketing of defective drug products. Between 1966 and 1971 alone, the Federal Drug Administration recalled nearly two thousand drug products, including "806 because of contaminations or adulterations, 752 because of subpotency or superpotency, and 377 because of label mixups" (Clinard and Yeager 1980, 266). Indeed, a study of seventeen pharmaceutical companies found that, over a two-year period each company violated the law once, and two drug companies committed more than twenty violations; when compared with other corporate sectors, the pharmaceutical companies committed two-and-one-half times their share of total violations (ibid., 120).

Two case examples are illustrative. Dr. William Sheddon, former vice-president and chief medical officer of Eli Lilly Research Laboratories, recently pleaded guilty to fifteen criminal counts relating to the marketing of Oraflex, an arthritis drug that has been linked to forty-nine deaths in the United States and several hundred worldwide, as well as thousands of cases of nonfatal liver and kidney failure. Sheddon was fined $15,000, and Lilly Research, which earned $3.1 billion in 1984, was fined $25,000 (Sherrill 1987, 50). Similarly Smith, Kline, Beckman Corporation "whizzed" their product Salacryn through the U.S. Food and Drug Administration with deadly results. Like Eli Lilly, they neglected to mention that their drug was a suspected killer. It had caused severe liver damage in some patients in France. False labels were used to market it in America, where it now is linked to thirty-six deaths and more than five hundred cases of liver and kidney damage (ibid., 50).

Women especially are victims of corporate pharmaceutical harm and violence. The drug Thalidomide produced enormous birth defects. Other drugs containing estrogen, progesterone and diethylstilbestrol (DES) are known to cause osteoporosis, heart disease, and defects in the circulatory and central nervous systems. Darvon, a mood-modifying drug, is highly overprescribed to women, especially the poor and the elderly, and simply sedates stress rather than eliminates it (Ford 1986; Harding 1986).

Another example of corporate exploitation of consumers' well-being surfaced in the exposé of the General Motors Corvair. From the beginning, the Corvair was troubled by rear-end suspension problems that caused it to become directionally unstable and unsafe at any speed. As revealed by John DeLorean, a GM executive of that time, "these problems with the Corvair were well documented inside GM's Engineering Staff long before the Corvair was offered for sale" (Wright 1979, 65). Nevertheless, the company marketed the Corvair, once again putting profits before safety, and resisted attempts by its own staff to introduce an inexpensive ($15 per vehicle) stabilizing bar capable of reducing the car's hazards. DeLorean offers a telling summation of corporate insensitivity and incorrigibility:

> To date [1979], millions of dollars have been spent in legal expenses and out-of-court settlements for those killed or maimed in the Corvair. The Corporation steadfastly defends the car's safety, despite the internal engineering records which indicated it was not safe, and the ghastly toll in deaths and injury it recorded (ibid, 67).

In addition to the dangers posed by consumer goods, it is estimated that annually 375,000 people in the developing world are poisoned — 10,000 of them fatally — through the exportation of hazardous and lethal chemicals (Michalowski and Kramer 1987, 38). In the United States an estimated "160 million tons of air pollution [are] emitted annually, [and] 225 million tons of toxic chemicals [are] discharged into waterways and streams" (Claybrook 1984, 118). The yearly national price tag of corporate disregard for the environment (including cleanup, lost production and medical fees) would be in the hundreds of billions of dollars. In the case of Allied Chemicals' unlawful discharge of the pesticide Kepone into the waterways of Virginia, the cleanup costs of the pollution alone totalled between $100 million and $2 billion (Fisse and Braithwaite 1983, 64).

In Canada, illegal dumping of waste products is common. Many millions of gallons of industrial waste and toxic chemicals have been thrown into sewers, ditches, rivers and lakes across the country. In January 1989, Inco Limited was fined $80,000 for releasing two tons of sulphur trioxide into the atmosphere from its Copper Cliff refinery in Ontario. The cloud of sulphuric acid one kilometre long and half a kilometre wide that formed, resulted in the hospitalization of 150 people. In March 1989 an Environment Canada report revealed that 83 of the 149 pulp mills in Canada were dumping toxic chemicals and poisonous dioxins into waterways at a rate and level above "allowable" standards. The pulp and paper industry was not investing in pollution control.

Canadian harbours are hideous repositories of wastes and poisons.

The Vancouver and Halifax harbours, for example, have high levels of lead, chromium, petroleum hydrocarbons, PCBs, benzopyrine and poly-nuclear aromatic hydrocarbons on their bottoms, and bottom-feeding fish have high rates of cancerous lesions and tumours. The local lobster fishery around the Sydney, Nova Scotia, harbour was closed in the early 1980s because of pollution caused by the leakage of transformer coolants into the water system (Gordon and Coneybeer 1991, 433). Dewey (1982, B1) notes:

> Canada lacks safe treatment for its hazardous wastes. For half a century, industry has been dumping potentially dangerous sub-stances into inadequately engineered landfills, many of which are now leaking. In some communities, leakages are being blamed for abnormal incidences of cancer, birth defects, and other health problems.

Approximately 10,000 underground storage tanks were leaking in Canada in 1989 and it was estimated that as many as 28,000 would leak over the following five years (Braul, Russell and Andrews 1989, 1).

The Sydney Steel Corporation (Sysco) case is infamous in Canada. For decades, Sysco has been dumping waste into "tar ponds" surround-ing its downtown Sydney, Nova Scotia, plant site. Now 700,000 tons of black toxic material, including cancer-causing polynuclear aromatic hydrocarbons and twenty other dangerous substances, are present in the "ponds." Despite a $34-million government cleanup operation, the predominantly working-class community in the vicinity of the plant has had higher than average cancer rates. Studies by the federal Bureau of Chemical Hazards and by Environment Canada revealed that the coke and steelmaking processes violated the provisions of the federal Clean Air Act in that emissions were between 2,800 and 6,000 percent above allowable standards and warned that coke-oven pollution would result in increases of morbidity and mortality in the community (Gordon and Coneybeer 1991, 438-39).

The words "Love Canal," in an ironic way, signify the severe damage that can be caused by toxic chemicals. For about ten years, the Hooker Chemical Company dumped 20,000 tons of chemical waste byproducts into a 15-acre trench located in Niagara Falls, New York. In 1953, William Love sold his dump site to the city's school board for a token $1.00, noting in the deed that the site was filled with chemical waste materials and transferring liability for injury and/or death to the new owner. Neither he nor the school board issued a public disclosure warning the public of the potential hazards. The land was eventually sold and used for residential housing and for educational purposes. Over the years the wastes seeped into the ground and its waters, with devastating consequences. Harmful solvents, pesticides and dioxins caused miscarriages, skin rashes, nervous disorders and high rates of cancer. Here is how Michael Brown (1979, XII) described the area in 1979:

> I saw homes where dogs had lost their fur. I saw children with serious birth defects. I saw entire families in inexplicably poor health. When I walked in the Love Canal, I gasped for air as my lungs heaved in fits of wheezing. My eyes burned. There was a sour taste in my mouth.

So severe was the danger that hundreds of families were evacuated, homes were bulldozed and parts of the Canal were closed off as uninhabitable (Albanese, 1984, 53).

A *Time* (October 14, 1985, 86) magazine article captures the insidiously silent means of environmentally produced harm and death:

> With the unnatural disasters caused by environmental toxins . . . the devastation is seldom certain or clear or quick. Broken chromosomes are unseen; carcinogens can be slow and sneaky. People wait for years to find out if they or their children are victims. The fears, the uncertainties and the conjectures have a corrosive quality that becomes inextricably mingled with the toxic realities.

Similarly, occupationally related diseases may be silent killers. As Staffman (1984, 16) notes, "these diseases usually do not appear until 20-40 years after exposure [and] are still causing the deaths of workers who laboured in the industry . . . before strict controls were imposed."

The mining industry not only claims the highest industrial fatality rate among workers, it also contributes heavily to injuries among the public. In 1982, for example, the Alcan Aluminum smelter in Kitimat, British Columbia, each day emitted 22 tons of sulphuric dioxide and between 1,000 to 2,000 pounds of hydrocarbon compounds. The result, aside from a dead zone a mile wide and 20 miles long, has been a clear and willful assault on the citizens of the town, all the more devastating because proper air pollution control technology has been available (Reason, Ross and Paterson 1981, 19, 20, 25; Goff and Reasons 1986, 217). According to Coleman (1989, 7), 90 percent of all cancers are environmentally induced by the illegal and legal toxins poured into the air, water and ground.

Clerical workers also suffer from exposure to toxic substances. The use of office equipment, such as photocopiers, requires the handling of various toxic powders and fluids. Asbestos insulation and products are a potential hazard, as are petrochemical products such as paints and poor carpeting, which emit poisonous gases. Poorly developed or improperly functioning ventilation systems in sealed buildings can cause pneumonitis, which is a buildup of bacteria in the cooling fluids of air conditioners that are then spread throughout the building. The term "sick building" is entirely appropriate to describe sealed edifices with inadequate fresh air and a buildup of hazardous gases and radiation (Reason, Ross and Paterson 1981; DeKeseredy and Hinch 1991, 111-12). Clerical workers increasingly risk cancers, respiratory diseases and damage to their reproductive health.

If avoidable consumer and citizen deaths and injuries were added to those of workers killed and assaulted in the workplace, then the ratio between corporate criminal violence and conventional criminal violence in Canada would be well in excess of 28:1. Henry (1986, 200) puts it as follows:

> In Canada each year there are about 500 victims of homicide; this compares with at least 15,000 Canadians who are killed each year as a result of the profit maximizing decisions of corporate executives.

Many attempts have been made to estimate the economic cost of corporate crime (Bequai 1978; Conklin 1977; Clinard and Yeager 1980; Ellis 1986; Michalowski,1985). But compiling reliable data on illegal monopoly pricing, transnational bribery and corruption, illegal mergers and takeovers, corporate tax evasion, misleading and fraudulent advertising, industrial pollution, crimes against worker safety, etc., is almost impossible. The invisibility of many of the crimes, the infrequency of reporting and detection, and the absence of any centralized data-collection agency have combined to preclude statistical accuracy (Casey 1985, 106-7; Michalos 1980, 34). A director for the Canadian Combines Investigation Act put it this way: "The informality of most complaints and the variety of subjects with which they deal create difficulties from the point of view of determining in the technical sense when an inquiry may fairly be said to exist" (Director of Investigations and Research 1965, 12). Snider (1978, 146) relates her research efforts as follows:

> Data-gathering was a lengthy and complicated procedure because the various regulatory agencies and government bodies

responsible for law enforcement and record keeping are extremely wary of releasing any facts.... Many of the statistics they gave could not be used because the same facts were not systematically gathered and presented each year, so comparisons were impossible. Or the categories would be so broad, combining so many parts of a by-law or statute, that the offences involving corporations or businesses could not be retrieved. Officials interviewed were loath to express opinions on anything, no matter how innocuous. Court records documenting who was charged and what sanctions were administered were private, not released to the general public.

At best, we have illustrative evidence that clearly understates the magnitude of the problem. However, one conclusion is not in dispute: persons are deprived of far more money by corporate crime than they are by conventional economic crimes, such as robbery, burglary, larceny and auto theft. Conklin (1977, 4) estimates that in 1977 these four offences in the USA accounted for about $4 billion, compared with the loss of almost $40 billion resulting from various crimes of capital, and this did not include environmental crime and crimes against workers' safety. A ratio of 10:1 would be a most conservative estimate of comparative economic loss. The data speak for themselves. Wheeler and Rothman (1982, 1414) found for the fiscal years 1976, 1977 and 1978 the median economic loss for white collar offenses committed by organizational offenders was $387,274. By contrast, the median take for white collar offenses committed on an individual basis was just in excess of $8,000. The gap becomes even more pronounced when street crime is considered.

The FBI statistics for 1984 indicate that the "average economic loss per crime was $689 for robbery, $900 for burglary, $376 for larceny-theft, and $4,418 for motor vehicle theft" (Cullen, Maakestad and Cavender 1987, 55). In the US, faulty goods, monopolistic practices and other economic violations are estimated to cost between $174 billion and $231 billion annually. One price-fixing case alone involving General Electric, Westinghouse and twenty-seven other electrical companies "cost utilities, and therefore the public, more money than is reported stolen in a year" (Clinard and Yeager 1980, 8). Costs are enormous: $35 million in overcharges in one area alone because of collusion by bread companies; $9 million in losses when dairy companies in one state set prices on the sale of milk to public schools; $225 million in losses as a result of a price-fixing by a blue-jeans company; untold millions of dollars extorted in overcharges caused by a massive bid-rigging scheme involving highway and paving contractors that led to fines totalling $50 million, 400 convictions and 141 prison sentences (Cullen, Maakestad and Cavender 1987, 60). Economic losses resulting from price-fixing in the plumbing industry cost $100 million; in the oil industry in one instance, nine major companies were sued for illegal overcharges of more than a billion dollars; in the securities market, one corporation Drexel Burnham, that pleaded guilty to insider trading has cost the U.S. taxpayer at least $500 billion dollars as well as anticipated tax hikes to cover the cost of bailing out the savings and loan industry. The economic losses to foreign governments has yet to be counted (ibid.; Snider 1991, 209-10).

Every year, it is estimated about $1.2 billion goes unreported in corporate tax returns, and violations of federal regulations result in annual losses to the taxpayer of between $10 billion and $20 billion (Clinard and Yeager 1980, 8). The huge economic losses that may result from a single corporate offender are exemplified by the fraud committed by the Equity Funding Corporation of America (EFCA). Through a strategy of separating exaggerated sales figures and profits, manipulating the value of company stock, laundering loans through foreign holdings, and eventually issuing totally fictitious policies for insurance benefits, EFCA stole $2 billion. Fifty to one hundred workers manufactured and sold 64,000 bogus policies and EFCA executives even "killed off" twenty-six "policyholders" and collected on their claims (Conklin 1977, 46). Similarly, E.F. Hutton's complex illegal check-kiting scheme involving over four hundred commercial banks resulted in a net illegal income of $10 billion; on some days, Hutton's company made $250 million in illegal "loans."

Banks have been convicted of failing to notify federal authorities of substantial cash deposits and foreign currency transactions, laundering money for organized crime, using illegal funds in investment and in interest-earning loans, and otherwise illegally accumulating profits. The First National Bank of Boston was fined $500,000 for failing to report illegal foreign transactions worth $1.2 billion (Cullen, Maakestad and Cavender 1987, 56). Susan Shapiro's (1984, 31-32) study of violations of financial trust investigated by the U.S. Securities and Exchange Commission (SEC) (e.g., stock manipulation, insider trading, stock value misrepresentation) shows that the mean cost to victims of SEC offenses was $100,000, with 19 percent of the cases incurring losses in excess of $500,000. For cases that end in criminal conviction, the costs are even higher. Wheeler and Rothman (1982, 1414-15) discovered that "the median take for a person convicted of SEC fraud was almost half a million dollars," and 20 percent of those cases were for losses in excess of $2.5 million.

More recently, corporations in the defense industry have been convicted of defrauding the taxpayer. From 1978 to 1981, General Dynamics defrauded the U.S. government of $7.5 million, and was later forced to settle $75 million in disputed overcharges. In May 1985, General Electric pleaded guilty to submitting $800,000 in false claims for payment on a missile contract. By 1986 more than fifty of the one hundred largest defense contractors were under criminal investigation (Cullen, Maakestad and Cavender 1987, 62-63).

In the United Kingdom, the employee pension funds of two public companies, Mirror Group Newspapers and Maxwell Communications Corporation, were siphoned off in an enormous illegal share-support scheme. At least £426 million (US$774 million) were raided from company pension funds, turned into cash and used to buy shares to prop up business losses and pay off bad loans. To date this is what is known:

Money Taken From	British £	US$
Mirror Group Newspapers pension fund	350 million	636 million
Other pension funds	76 million	138 million
Mirror Group Newspapers PLC	97 million	176 million
Maxwell Communications Corp.	240 million	436 million
Total	763 million	1,386 million
Transferred To		
Buy Maxwell Communications shares	300 million	545 million
Provide collateral for bank loans on private companies	150 million	272 million
Pay a pension obligation to a printing company	100 million	182 million
Pay interest on private company loans	80 million	145 million
Total	630 million	1,144 million

Nor is this the whole story. An estimated £600 million (US$1,690 million) is still not accounted for, and the size of this illegal share scam may well exceed £1 billion (*Globe and Mail*, December 9 and 10, 1991).

In Canada, failure to remit payroll deductions by employers alone "accounted for $7.9 million, while bank robbers, extortionists and kidnappers gained a profit of only $5.17 million" (Goff and Reasons 1978, 11). Sears Canada made $7 million profit by selling improperly appraised diamond rings to Canadian consumers (Goff and Reasons 1986, 209). More generally, in Canada, the total economic cost of corporate workplace violence alone is thought to range between $5.7 billion and $20.9 billion, or between 1.7 and 6.3 percent of the Canadian gross national product (GNP) (Ellis 1986, 96).

Whether we are workers, consumers or citizens, we stand far more chance of being robbed, injured or killed by upstanding, "law-abiding" citizens who roam corporate suites than by those who haunt public streets. The social consequences of this staggering exploitation should not be underestimated. As Cullen, Maakestad and Cavender (1987, 65) observe:

> Corporations damage the quality of social life.... Through illegal labor practices ranging from safety violations to wage discrimination, they make the "good life" less attainable for their employees at work and at home. Through illegal pollution of air and water, they rob the general public of healthy and pleasing surroundings and of enjoyable recreational facilities.

Corporate irresponsibility may lead to the complete elimination of communities, such as in Buffalo Creek, West Virginia, where a poorly constructed mining company dam collapsed and unleashed 130 million gallons of water and coal waste. One hundred and twenty-five people were drowned or crushed to death, one thousand homes were destroyed and sixteen small communities were washed away. The words of one survivor are haunting:

> We lost many things we loved, and we think about those things. We think about our neighbors and friends we lost. Our neighborhood was completely destroyed, a disaster area. There's just an open field there now and grass planted where there were many homes and many people lived (quoted in Erikson 1976, 196).

Similarly, in Canada, Native peoples have been especially susceptible to community destruction brought about by corporate greed and irresponsibility. Anastasia Shkilnyk (1985, 202) in her book on the Grassy Narrows reserve in Ontario, has shown how mercury poisoning delivered a major blow to the Indian way of life when the fishing and guide camps were forced to close down. The economic loss to this community over a fifty-year period (1970-2020) is estimated to be more than $3 million. Moreover, the environmental poisoning has wreaked havoc on the moral, political and psychic character of the community, leaving in its wake a shattered society of broken lives. The testimony of Dr. Prichard, an established neurologist with experience in methyl mercury poisoning, is instructive:

> The people of Grassy Narrows have had a rough time. . . . They have had to change the location of their reserve, they have been regimented into hideous little houses. They've love fishing, its been their life and someone has said, "you can't fish." They've had all kinds of problems with alcohol and drugs. And on this background, they've had this horrible thing of someone saying, 'you can't eat the fish, they'll poison you. And not only that, but the fish you have eaten probably have poisoned you, and you probably are dying." It's an appalling thing (ibid., 199).

The political economy of resource extraction and development — for coal, uranium, oil, forestry products, hydro-electric power and water — have severely dislocated the Lubicon of northern Alberta, the Cree of Quebec, the Haida of British Columbia, the Metis of Manitoba and the Cree of northern Saskatchewan, to name a few. Native communities have been depressed, demoralized and destroyed as hydro-electric and radioactive colonization has turned their lands, resources and villages into dumping grounds for toxic wastes or flooded them out of existence (Richardson 1989; LaDuke 1990; Harding 1989; Waldram 1988). So severe is the damage caused by corporate exploitation that the Native peoples of the "entire northern half of the Americas stand in imminent danger of being swallowed up and eliminated entirely" (Churchill and LaDuke 1991, 42).

Two community studies are illustrative. The first concerns the Aluminum Company of Canada and the Carrier people of Cheslatta Lake in British Columbia. In 1952, Alcan began the construction of its huge aluminum smelter in Kitimat, British Columbia. The project was entirely dependent upon harnessing hydro-electric power, thus giving rise to the Kemano project, which involved building the Kenney Dam across the Nechako River which in turn flooded lakes and tributary river systems. River flows were reversed and diverted west towards Kemano, and their powerful energy was channelled to Alcan's giant turbines via a tunnel bored through a mountain. This was an engineering feat of unprecedented magnitude.

But there were casualties. The plan involved cutting off water to the Nechako River until a 890-kilometre reservoir was flooded in place above the dam site. This meant that the lucrative salmon run could not migrate up the river system. Alcan decided that a second temporary dam should be built on nearby Murray Lake, thus creating an ancillary reservoir to keep the Nechako River primed with water while the larger reservoir gradually filled up. The river would live and the fish would survive. But a new dam meant even more flooding, and just upstream from Murray Lake was Cheslatta Lake and the Native community of Cheslatta which stood to be eliminated by the hydro-electric project.

Here is a record, in outline, of what happened to the Cheslatta Natives:

- On April 3, 1952, the Native people were advised by Alcan and the federal Department of Indian Affairs that their lands were going to be flooded.
- On April 8th, Alcan began flooding Murray Lake and by extension Cheslatta Lake even though they had no license to "store and divert." This permit eventually was issued after the fact on July 21st and backdated to April 2nd.
- On April 20th and 21st, the Native community was told to surrender their lands for compensation. Tactics used included designating a government-appointed chief and two councillors as the band leaders and "negotiating" a deal with them, as well as forging Native signatures and deceiving the community about the compensation package. In the end, Alcan paid $129,000 for 1,050 hectares of land, far less than was originally promised.
- On April 22nd, the Native community was forced to move about 50 kilometres away to Grassy Plains under the most arduous of spring travelling conditions. They were forced to leave behind livestock and personal property.
- Shortly thereafter, contractors hired by Alcan burned the Native villages to the ground, thus preventing any possible return by the Natives to their homeland.
- For years following the flooding and the "surrender" of their lands, the Cheslatta Natives tried to eke out a living on the scattered parcels of land at Grass Plains. Their formerly cohesive and orderly community became a dependent, despondent and demoralized group of people. Suicide, alcoholism and "welfarism" all increased as a result of the alienation from their land.

- Native burial grounds were desecrated. Alcan moved a handful of recent graves but burned the coffins, remains and markers of the others they found. A plaque was erected to the memory of the dead now under water. On May 7, 1957, after the worst flooding was over, seventeen graves were completely washed away. Bones, bodies and coffins were found floating in the lake or washed up on the shores.

- In the early 1980s the Cheslatta Natives confronted the government of Canada with their grievances. They demanded the full compensation they had been promised. They wanted recognition that the federal government had not protected their interests at the time of the land surrender and demanded to be allowed to return to their homeland and redevelop it as best they could, given that Murray Lake Dam had long since been removed.

- The government of Canada twice refused the claims of the Cheslatta band, but then in 1984 it agreed to accept a specific claim. Negotiations proceeded for six years without resolution.

- In 1989, Alcan agreed to return most of the land that it had taken from the Cheslatta people thirty-seven years before. But there was a condition: a Kemano II project must be allowed to go forward. So the irony is that the Natives were asked to agree to more hydro-electric colonization in order to have their lands returned to them, which is why they were forced to surrender the lands in the first place.

- In the process of pursuing and negotiating their claims with Alcan and the federal government, forgeries were discovered. To date, ninety-two signatures on fifty-six surrender and compensation documents are alleged to be forged. A forensic expert now claims that the ninety-two X's said to have been marked by Natives were in fact the work of one person, so far unknown.

- In 1990, after delays and negotiation setbacks, the Cheslatta Natives launched a federal court suit against the government, demanding that the land surrender and transfer to Alcan be declared null and void and set aside and that the court award damages to the people of the Cheslatta reserves. In March 1991, the government's statement of defense rebutted virtually every claim. The case now rests in legal limbo (Waldram 1988, 15-17; Cheslatta Band 1991b, 1-7; Cheslatta Band 1991a, 1-18).

The Navajo nation in the United States, the Kerr-McGee Mining Corporation and the U.S. Atomic Energy Commission represent the principal actors in the second community study. In 1952 the Navajo Tribal Council approved a mineral extraction agreement with Kerr-McGee. In return for jobs, royalties and economic development, the

Navajo permitted access to uranium deposits on the reservation. From 1952 to 1980, the Shiprock facility was mined and the ore was sent, for the most part, to the U.S. Atomic Energy Commission. One hundred and fifty Navajo men were trained and hired to work in underground operations, but, by 1975, eighteen had died of radiation-induced lung cancer. By 1980, another twenty had died of this disease and a further ninety-five had contacted similar respiratory ailments and cancers. Birth defects such as cleft palate and leukemia had risen dramatically in Shiprock and downstream Navajo communities. Worker safety regulations had been frequently abrogated. Ventilation units were not always in operation and one report dating from 1959 noted radiation levels in the Kerr-McGee facility to be ninety times the allowable limit. Lax safety enforcement underground was compounded by waste dumping aboveground, where the corporation left behind some 71 acres of raw uranium tailings, which retained 85 percent of the original radioactivity of the ore, stored only some sixty feet from the San Juan River. The results are not surprising: continuing radioactive contamination of the major water source and the surrounding downstream habitat and inhabitants (Churchill and LaDuke 1991; Churchill,1991).

The political economy of hydroelectric and radioactive colonialism is far more extensive than these two examples suggest. The "expendability" of the indigenous population under the banner of corporate profit and progress, the public interest, the common good, and civilization has been enormous. The Hopi in Arizona, the Lakota in Montana and North Dakota, the Sioux in South Dakota, the Klamath in Oregon, the Cree in Quebec, the Objibwa in Ontario, the Cree and Chipewan in Alberta, the Carrier-Sekanie and the Gitksan-We'tsewu'tan in British Columbia, and the Metis and Cree peoples of Manitoba and Saskatchewan all have had their lands, resources, economies, friends, families and future genera-tions "sacrificed" for corporate development. Their communities have been terminated as their lands have been flooded, stolen and "nuked." Long the victims of corporate and government criminal abuse, they now risk becoming "the first twentieth century national sacrifice peoples" in what seems like a callous corporate plan of annihilation (Churchill and LaDuke 1991; Waldram 1988).

While predatory street crime corrodes the fabric of social life, crimes of capital such as these fracture, in very profound ways, the economic and political systems. They not only call into question the moral conduct of business and the quality of social life, but they bolster fundamental inequalities within and between nation-states. Stock manipulations and frauds undermine public investment and confidence in capital (Conklin 1977, 7), and bribes, corruption, land frauds, kickbacks, environmental degradation and the dumping of hazardous wastes undercut political institutions. As Braithwaite (1979b, 126) observes, the problem is global:

> Transnational corporate corruption is therefore perhaps the most pernicious form of crime in the world today because it involves robbing the poor to feed the rich, and brings into political power rulers and administrators who in general put self-interest ahead of public interest, and transnational corporation interest ahead of national interest.

Consider the case of Bhopal, India. On the night of December 2, 1984, water entered into a methyl isocyanate (MIC) storage tank, setting in process an exothermic reaction that led to a buildup of pressure that ruptured the tank. Gases burst forth into the atmosphere and caused the world's worst industrial disaster. The devastation was sudden and immense. The death toll is estimated to be between 1,754 (the official Indian government figure) and 10,000. Almost a quarter of a million people were exposed to the toxic gases, more than 60,000 were severely injured and about 20,000 were permanently handicapped. No evacuation or safety plan was in place. The explosion destroyed entire communities and severely disrupted family life (Pearce and Tombs 1989, 117).

Officials of Union Carbide India Limited (UCIL), the local subsidiary of Union Carbide Corporation (UCC), immediately declared that the plant met the same safety standards as its American and other overseas operations: "In India or Brazil or someplace else . . . same equipment, same design, same everything" (Everest 1986, 47-48). In the year immediately following the disaster, UCC repeatedly denied responsibility and blamed the government and the political culture of India, which it said was "backward," unstable and liable to violent industrial espionage. Indeed, throughout the lengthy legal process, Union Carbide lawyers and executives claimed that the disaster was sabotage and hence not the company's legal responsibility.

The facts, however, belie the company's claims. Consider the following:

- equipment was badly maintained,
- temperatures of gases and leaks were not logged,
- spare parts were lacking,
- the staff was untrained,
- the plant design as a whole was faulty,
- plant instruments were inadequate to monitor normal production processes and leaks were detected by smell only,

- the refrigeration plant was not powerful enough to cool all of the MIC stored,
- local medical services and the state and national governments were not informed fully as to the nature and effects of the deadly gaseous emissions,
- UCC withheld information on the dangers of the MIC production process from UCIL, and both withheld information from the Indian state, the plant workers and the local communities,
- warnings from trade unions and local journalists about production dangers and risks to health, safety and environment were ignored or distrusted by UCC and UCIL,
- regulatory agencies were under-resourced and overwhelmed by the professional and technical expertise of UCIL, and
- corporate engineers overexaggerated claims to safety and predictability, held an arrogant belief in their own views and an indifference to other viewpoints, and miscalculated the risks and thus contributed to misinformation about plant production processes (Pearce and Tombs 1989, Everest 1986).

On February 14, 1989, Union Carbide Corporation and the Indian state reached a final settlement. Instead of receiving $3.3 billion, the victims of the Bhopal tragedy received $470 million. Union Carbide was immune from all impending litigation, including criminal charges. The money was used to compensate the families of the 3,329 "officially recognized dead" and the more than 20,000 seriously injured. Insurance was to cover about $200 million of the damages awarded, and the rest would be accounted for by a special retroactive levy of 50 cents on 1988 shareholders' dividends. The $270 million levy was to be small in comparison to the $1 billion bonus paid out to shareholders in 1986 (Pearce and Tombs 1989, 138).

Union Carbide got off lightly. It did not have to prove its claims of sabotage, had no liability and did not have to accept responsibility for the poor design and condition of the Bhopal plant. At best, as Everest (1986) notes: "a Bhopal resident, whose wife was killed, whose lungs are permanently scarred and is unable to work and whose children suffer from psychological trauma may end up with $20,000." In the end, the industrial and political strength of the transnational Union Carbide chemical firm overwhelmed the Indian government and the people of Bhopal. As Pearce and Tombs (1989, 139) aptly conclude, "the settlement is clearly a political one, imposed by international capital and the major imperialist power."

From the evidence presented above, it should be obvious that corporate crime should be a major concern of critical criminology, which should address why corporate crime is so endemic, what has been done to control it, and what alternative policy initiatives may be taken. Before explaining corporate crime, it is helpful to order our discussion and examples into a coherent typology. As we have seen, corporate crime is diverse, as well as costly and harmful. It occurs in the home, in neighbourhoods and at the workplace. It is so pervasive that it cannot be ascribed to misguided individuals who somehow went down the "wrong corporate corridor." We have implied that corporate crime is a structural problem, "built into" the business economy. I do not mean to say that all corporate executives and associates are criminals, but rather that the pressures for profitability are strong and enduring and bear upon the routine responses of corporations in areas where risk and uncertainty are high and where resources are valuable. Nor am I stating that such crime happens only in capitalist economies. Clearly, harm and homicide like those discussed above can and do occur in so-called socialist states, as the Chernobyl nuclear disaster illustrates, and crimes of capital may occur in developing capitalist societies, where exploitation is equally severe and oppression even greater than in developed industrial societies. But the logics of explaining the social, physical and economic costs of such activities and enterprises comparatively are different and require a separate analysis.

For our purposes, five types of corporate crime in Western democratic societies may be identified (Bequai 1978; Box 1983; Braithwaite 1979b; Coleman 1989; Ermann and Lundman 1978b, 1982; Goff and Reasons 1986; Michalowski 1985; Snider 1978, 1988; Gordon and Coneybeer 1991):

1. against consumers (false advertising; false labelling of products; production and distribution of untested and harmful goods; misleading sales information and behaviour; selling goods at overinflated prices; dumping inferior and adulterated products on Third World markets; failure or delay in correcting known product hazards; misuse of credit information),
2. against the public and the environment (air, water and land pollution; unwarranted depletion of valuable scarce resources; bribery and corruption to undermine public trust and institutions; increasing the public tax bill by means of corporate tax avoidance schemes or by fraudulent means; destruction of entire communities and their ways of living),
3. against workers (refusal to make work environments, condi-

tions and procedures safe; refusal to properly carry out inspections and site maintenance; paying under the table to avoid employee benefits; paying wages below the legal allowable limit; concealing information from workers about work-related disease or injury; refusing to recognize, sabotaging and harassing democratically elected unions; pension fund abuse),

4. against corporate competitors (price-fixing to force out competitors or to rationalize existing competition; insider trading and stock fraud; mergers or takeovers in violation of anticombines legislation; industrial espionage and corporate sabotage; arson, patent fraud and cheating; blackmail, bribery, influence peddling, and corruption to affect developing or expanding markets and regulators), and

5. against the state (fraudulent contract billing of government departments; tax evasion and avoidance; supplying illegal campaign funds to politicians or political parties in return for favours and sponsorship; bribing state officials; organizing, aiding or abetting misinformation to halt, modify or repeal regulations and legislation; exporting illegal behaviour to other nations and states.

We now know the what, the where and the who of corporate crime, but the unanswered questions are how and why it is possible for corporate lawlessness to be so widespread. In answering these questions we need to examine the relationship between economy, bureaucracy, state and law. As Hills (1987,190) notes, "the key to understanding corporate crime lies . . . in the culture and structure of large-scale bureaucratic organizations within a particular political economy."

• 3 •
Capital Accumulation, Corporate Bureaucracy and Corporate Crime

Corporate crime and other crimes of capital arise from processes of capital accumulation and growth (McBarnett 1982,157-60). The starting point of analysis is an understanding of the dynamic of capital and capital accumulation. We can define *capital* as something of value that may be exchanged for something of greater value. *Value* can be of two types: use value and exchange value. *Use value* corresponds to the ability of a product to fulfill a specific need, as when a carpenter produces a bed to sleep on at night for her own comfort. *Exchange value* resides in a relationship of equivalence "in which values in use of one sort are exchanged for those of another sort" (Marx 1973, 36). Should the carpenter decide to make beds to trade for grain or fuel, then the value of the bed for the carpenter is transformed from a use value to an exchange value. The carpenter no longer values the bed for its comfort, but because it enables her to acquire other commodities. This is an important transformation. The initial product that was characterized as having use value was inherently unequal to other products and their use value. It had no measure of equivalency for purposes of exchange. However, once an object is produced to be transferred to another for the other's use value, it becomes a *commodity* (ibid., 1973, 40-41). It enters into a relation of quantitative exchange in which two products are brought into a proportional relationship (e.g., two beds equals ten wool blankets).

This ratio of exchange finds advanced expression in the development of a third commodity that is recognized as an equivalent measure of value: money. Whether as livestock, shells, coins or paper, *money* is a symbolic representation of a thing's worth that can be applied to all commodities. Money serves as a universal equivalent of value. By our example, if two beds are worth $100, so are ten wool blankets. Qualitatively distinct commodities can enter a relationship in the marketplace where an abstract system of equivalences prevails. Beds may be exchanged for money, which in turn may be exchanged for blankets. The possibilities for exchange and trade are widened as the money nexus draws ever more individuals into an increasing number of commodity exchanges. Money comes to replace the value of all commodities. At this point, "the memory of use-value, as distinct from exchange-value, has become entirely extinguished in this incarnation of pure exchange value" (ibid., 239-40). Money also makes possible exchange for its own sake. Instead of selling in order to buy, one can now buy in order to sell. Trade emerges as a specialized activity in itself, the raison d'être being the acquisition of money. It is precisely when money is set upon a course of exchange with the primary objective of realizing more money that it becomes capital. Thus, when a trader buys linen for $10 in order to sell it later or elsewhere for $15, he is buying to sell for profit. He will acquire *surplus value* in the form of more money through the act of exchange than he had initially. The realization of surplus value through repeated acts of buying and selling for profit makes possible even greater accumulated value, and this is the process of the *accumulation of capital*.

The money-commodity-money relation then is the fundamental component of the circulation of capital within a capitalist economy. But, more than a medium of circulation, money also facilitates the management of wealth on a massive scale. Money permits the acquisition or disposal of goods between persons who are widely separated in space and time. In a fully fledged capitalist economy, the combination of sophisticated recordkeeping and accounting, and the provision of credit facilities — the core of banking — make possible a rational calculus of profit over long spans of time and space and a system of storage of value whereby obligations may be manipulated against future promises of payment (Weber 1978, 80).

But what is the basis of value? What makes things in nature such as trees, coal, iron ore, and diamonds valuable? The answer is labour power. The appropriation and transformation of nature-given materials by human labour power imparts value to objects. The production of value through labour is a social process, particularly so in industrialized societies where the production of value for most commodities involves an elaborate division and coordination of labour. But the value created by the social act of labouring is subject to different modes of production and distribution. In some systems of production, surplus is either shared equally or retained collectively by the society as a whole as a compensation against future hard times (as in egalitarian societies). In other modes of production, owners expropriate the entire product of labour, returning to the producer the bare minimum of food and shelter (as in slave economies), or they acquire a large proportion of the social surplus by appropriating the products of unpaid labour that peasants were required to give as part of their feudal bonds (as in feudal societies). In either case, a possessing class exploits labour power and retains for itself a disproportionate share of the value produced (Giddens 1981, 109-23).

Under capitalism, the value produced by labour is controlled by the segment of society with the capital to buy labour power. The process of exploitation is not based on forced labour or corvée labour. Nor is exploitation naked and direct under capitalism. It is a hidden process. The structural set is money-labour-contract-profit, that is, capital privately appropriates the social product by extracting surplus value through wage labour in a "free" labour market. Surplus value is extracted when the value produced by labour is more than the value returned to labour in the form of wages and benefits. Stated another way, the logic of capital is to buy labour power for wages less than the value that will be produced by this labour. Labour power itself becomes a commodity, a cost to capital, but by expending labour power the worker creates added value when she continues to work past the time at which production is equivalent to wages. This difference between value paid for the value produced is the surplus. For example, the essence of doing business is to pay Worker X $100 a week for a job at which she is really producing value at $200 a week. The principle, as with money-commodity-money is to buy in order to sell for a profit. For this to happen, Worker X must provide the employer with a certain amount of "free" labour (i.e., one-half a week's worth). It is "free" because the employer is appropriating it as profit rather than returning it back to the worker (Marx 1973).

What then is done with the profit? It can be used by owners and managers of capital to finance consumption of use value for personal use (e.g., cars, jewels, art, real estate) or it can be transformed into capital by returning it to finance further profit-making activities. Usually both processes occur with a balance being struck between corporate reinvestment, stock dividends and private consumption (Baran and Sweezy 1966, 39-40). Stockholders, of course, may in turn use their dividends for private, even conspicuous consumption, or they may use them as capital for possible future profit growth (ibid., 1966, 16-17). The basic function of business from its origins to the present has been and remains profit expansion. Even the advent of a professional managerial class that administers the allocation of capital for those who own capital has not altered the fact that "the giant corporation of today is an engine for maximizing profits and accumulating capital" (ibid., 1966, 47).

The pressure to extract surplus value continually and to increase productivity derives from the competitive character of capitalism and its need for constant capital accumulation. This has tended to favour central-ization and concentration of capital. As the corporation developed as the basic organization of capital, it shed many of its social and public service functions, becoming almost exclusively a money-making enterprise (Snider 1988, 233). In order to survive economically — to stave off bankruptcy and takeovers by competitors — corporations have in-creased in size and power. In Canada, through a combination of horizon-tal and vertical integrations, conglomerate mergers and intercorporate directorates, the economy has come to be dominated by a diminishing number of corporations.

The number of mergers climbed from 186 in 1959 to 504 in 1969, declined to 264 in 1975 and then jumped to 398 in 1977, 449 in 1978 and 511 in 1979 (Veltmeyer 1987, 28, 29, 43). The number of *dominant* corporate enterprises declined from 170 in 1951 to 113 in 1972 (Clement 1975, 125-50). By 1983, a mere twenty-five dominant enterprises composed of 585 corporations accounted for 34 percent of all industrial assets (i.e., build-ings, land, equipment and other property), 23.5 percent of all sales and 32.6 percent of all nonfinancial corporate profit. The top 100 enterprises, which controlled 1,398 of 397,965 corporations, accounted for more than one-third of sales and more than 50 percent of all industrial assets and profits.

If we look more closely on a sector by sector basis, we find the degree of concentration in 1983 to be staggering. In the manufacturing sector, corporations with assets of $25 million or more (only 2 percent of all manufacturing corporations) accounted for 79.1 percent of all manufac-turing assets, 72.3 percent of all sales and 68.9 percent of all profits. In mining, four corporations accounted for 47.3 percent of all sales, and eight for 67.3 percent of all profits. In primary metals the top eight corporations accounted for 83.3 percent of all assets, 74.2 percent of sales and 67.4 percent of profits. In the petroleum industry, the big four — Exxon (Imperial Oil), Shell, Texaco and Gulf — controlled 64 percent of Canadian refining capacity and 58 percent of retail outlets. In 1983, four firms accounted for more than 90 percent of the output of tobacco products, beer and ale, and automobiles. In twenty other industries, including iron and steel, cement, and aluminum, four firms accounted for 75 percent of production. In banking, the five largest banks controlled $207 billion, or 90 percent of the assets of all federally chartered banks. Today the situation is such that just twelve families and five conglomerates control over one-third of all corporate assets (Francis 1986; Marchak 1988, 60-71; Veltmeyer 1987, 18, 23-25, 32, 44).

The size of corporations has also mammothly increased. Transnational corporations (TNCs) often exceed the economies of nation-states. The World Bank and *Fortune* magazine estimate that among the top one hundred economies in the world, forty-six are corporate entities, each having sales that outstrip the gross national product of more than 150 countries. General Motors and Exxon have combined company sales of $183.1 billion, more than the combined GNPs of Sweden and Switzerland. Royal Dutch/Shell, ranked twenty-third with sales of $81.7 billion, exceeds the economies of Indonesia ($80.6 billion), Belgium ($77.6 billion), Argentina ($76.2 billion), Poland ($75.4 billion), South Africa ($73.4 billion), and Austria ($64.5 billion). What is particularly alarming is that the numbers and revenues of TNCs are increasing at two to three times national rates of growth. In the twenty years from 1960 to 1980, the revenues of transnational corporations grew tenfold from $199 billion to $2,155 billion. By 1983 the worldwide profits of TNCs had reached a high of $130 billion (Cavanaugh and Clairmonte 1983, 17). The prognosis was that by 1991 these corporations would account for two-thirds of the nonsocialist world's industrial output and four-fifths of its productive assets (Veltmeyer 1987, 77-79).

Within Canada, the growth of TNCs has resulted in intrusive U.S. and other foreign control of the Canadian economy, especially in the resource extraction and manufacturing sectors, and increased concentrations of economic power. Consider the following examples of Canadian capital concentration:

- Westons: control more than 700 companies worldwide; in Canada alone a group of 160 companies with visible assets and sales of about $9 billion.
- Thomsons: major players in the newspaper market and in retail merchandising, worth $8 billion; controlling interests in Hudson's Bay Co., Simpson's and Zeller's, as well as 50 percent control of the newspaper market in Canada.
- Conrad Black and Paul Desmarais - two intercorporate empires that combine some of Canada's largest industrial corporations, merchandisers, and investment firms. Together these two groups control a total of 350 corporations and through their subsidiaries a further 1,500 companies, with total combined assets of $60 billion.
- Bronfmans: a family group that controls a business empire that includes financial services, liquor distilling, real estate, min-

ing, forestry and oil exploration; the intercorporate network is said to have assets of nearly $60 billion (Francis 1986; Marchak 1988; Veltmeyer 1987).

The centralization and concentration of capital means that productive facilities become larger and less in number. Fewer and fewer private individuals control and decide the use of ever larger amounts of capital, and larger numbers of people become dependent upon single corporate enterprises that are not accountable to an electorate. As Marchak (1988, 71-72) notes,

> in Canada [corporations] are not even required to report fully their financial standing. They make decisions that affect not only their shareholders . . . and not only their employees . . . but the entire population, and the economic environment and the political possibilities of the entire nation (indeed of many nations). Yet they make these public decisions in private and with reference to private goals and private profit."

Not surprisingly, the ownership of wealth in Canada was and remains highly concentrated. The richest 2 percent of the population holds nearly one-third of the total wealth of Canada. Their income is not derived mainly from wages but is accumulated from investment and inheritance profits. In 1983, about 9,363 individuals reported taxable incomes over $250,000. Less than 0.5 percent of Canadian taxpayers (a total of 55,147 individuals) had incomes of more than $100,000, and about 4.4 percent of the 15,302,940 Canadian taxpayers paid taxes on income of $50,000 or more (ibid., 30).

In the United States the pattern is roughly similar. The top 500 corporations control 75 percent of all manufacturing assets; 50 out of 67,000 companies in transportation and utilities control 66 percent of the airline, railway, electricity and gas, and communications industries; three corporations account for most of the revenues and assets in television; and four firms control the movie industry; two insurance conglomerates control 25 percent of the industry, and 50 of the remaining 1,890 corporations control three-quarters of the remaining market; 50 out of 17,700 banks control more than three-fifths of all banking assets, and three of these banks control about 20 percent of these assets (Simon and Eitzen 1986, 10). By 1983 the annual sales of the 500 largest corporations exceeded US$1.7 trillion and by 1985 the revenues of the top five corporations (General Motors, Exxon, Royal Dutch/Shell, Mobil and Ford Motor) totalled $373.6 billion, more than the GNP of the entire U.S. economy (Coleman 1989, 12-14; Veltmeyer 1987, 78-79).

The richest one percent own 25 percent of the combined market worth of everything owned by every American. Indeed, less than 0.5 percent of the total population "own about 80 percent of all corporate stock and 90 percent of all tax-exempt state and local bonds." Within this already limited group is a small but highly integrated group of super-rich, "about one twentieth of 1 percent of the total population, who own 20 percent of *all* corporate stock, 66 percent of *all* state and local bonds, and 40 percent of *all* other bonds and notes" (Michalowski 1985, 323).

The process of extraction of surplus value, the competitive drive for the accumulation of capital, and the centralization and concentration of capital and wealth have a direct bearing on the evolution and character of the corporation as a criminal actor. As Braithwaite (1991, 45) observes, "capital can be used to constitute illegitimate opportunities and the more capital the bigger the opportunities." Unlike that of the poor, whose criminality is often motivated by a desire for goods for use or a fear of losing goods for use, the criminal conduct of the rich is frequently guided by exchange motivations. Surplus can be used intentionally to constitute a range of criminal possibilities — by setting up tax evasion schemes, defrauding investors or consumers, fixing prices on markets, setting up illegal businesses in drugs or arms — in a way that income for use cannot. The "resource holding potential" of capital allows its holders enormous access to money, to expertise (e.g., lawyers, accountants, politicians), to organizations through which capital flows, and to counter-strategy powers to thwart investigation, apprehension and prosecution (Cohen and Marchalek 1988).

Many studies show that large national and transnational corporations are the chief violators. Sutherland (1973, 80), in his pioneering work in 1948, stated that 98 percent of the corporations he studied could be considered recidivists, bearing two or more adverse decisions. Using four convictions as a measure, he found that "90 percent of the 70 largest corporations in the United States are habitual criminals." Clinard and Yeager's (1980, 119) research on industrial capital discovered that "small corporations accounted for only one-tenth of the violations, medium sized for one-fifth, but larger corporations for almost three-fourths of all violations, nearly twice their expected percentage." Large and integrated corporate conglomerates are more likely to be multiple offenders, averaging about five violations. Furthermore, they accounted for 72.1 percent of the serious and 62.8 percent of the moderately serious violations (ibid., 1980, 119-20).

Illegalities were most common in the highly concentrated and centralized oil, pharmaceutical and automobile industries, which together had anywhere from 2.5 to 3.9 times their share of total violations. Indeed, the auto industry had five times its share of serious and moderately serious cases. Seller concentration, buyer concentration, entry barriers, price elasticity, and corporate growth policies are market conditions especially conducive to corporate crime (Conklin 1977, 51-52). The twenty-nine electrical equipment industry companies convicted of price-fixing controlled 95 percent of the market. The bulk of product production was in few hands, the demand for the product was price-inelastic and market entry barriers such as capital investment, sophisticated technical skills and patent rights were in place (ibid.; Geis 1978). Similar studies on the automobile industry by Leonard and Weber (1970), on the pharmaceutical industry (Braithwaite 1984), on corporate tax fraud (Conklin 1977, 67) on oil refining and production (Canada 1981) and on combines legislation (Snider 1978) confirm that "dominant" or large firms are actively and routinely breaking the law. Bowles and Edwards (1985, 88) have likened capitalism to a "race" where winners and losers enter, gain, fall behind or drop out. Then new firms enter afresh, and even the leaders must worry about this potential competition. Clearly the rules of the race do not preclude cheating to get ahead.

Nowhere is this more obvious than in developing countries where giant corporations have relocated their industrial facilities in the expectation that labour, environmental, consumer and regulatory climates will be nonrestrictive. Not surprisingly, they have exported many of the hazards and harms of industrial production: safety and health problems, pollution and dangerous wastes, injurious consumer products, and political bribery and corruption. As Michalowski and Kramer (1987, 36) observe, "the growing internationalization of business points to developing nations as a significant emerging arena for injurious corporate activity." The fatal poisoning of thousands of residents of Bhopal, India, dramatized that when problems do occur, the human and environmental costs are likely to be greater than those resulting from similar incidents in developed countries. For example, perhaps the best-known example of irresponsible marketing involved the sale of baby formula to the inhabitants of Third World nations. The sale of this product by Nestle was alleged to have caused the death of 10,000 babies per year. Nestle campaigned to convince women not to breast-feed so that they would buy baby formula — its marketing strategy was to foster a dependency on the product. However, the company did not consider that poor parents had to mix formula with available water sources because product costs were too high for them. Impurities in the water supplies and the high cost of the formula led to product dilution and resulted in many thousands of cases of infant starvation (Simon and Eitzen 1986).

The dynamic of capital accumulation and profit maximization takes place within the organizational context of the corporate bureaucracy.

Here the goals and principles of profit-making are translated into a set of specific official directives that set forth both what the corporation says it is doing and what it is actually doing, regardless of announced aims (Perrow 1961, 1972). The need to succeed in the attainment of corporate goals shapes the activities of the corporation to competitors, employees, governments and consumers. These organizational goals, embedded within the operative structure and ideology of the corporation contain an "inherent inducement" or an "invitational edge" to engage in crime (Gross 1978,56; Hagan 1987, 329). Braithwaite (1991, 45) succinctly observes:

> most capital investment simultaneously constitutes a range of both legitimate and illegitimate means of further increasing the wealth of the capitalist. The wealth that creates legal opportunities at the same time brings illegal opportunities for achieving the same result into existence.

And Gross (1978, 57) puts it as follows:

> Given a situation of uncertainty in attaining goals, and one in which the organization is judged (directly, or indirectly by sales or other indicators) by its success in goal attainment or performance, one can predict that the organization will, if it must, engage in criminal behaviour to attain these goals.

For example, the contradiction between corporate goal achievement and environmental risks creates a strong impetus towards "innovative behaviour which can stretch over the spectrum [of] law-abiding - law avoiding - law evading - law breaking" (Box 1983, 36).

Following this perspective, Snider (1988), Box (1983), Kramer (1982) and Braithwaite (1984, 1991) argue that corporate criminality is directly related to primary business goals, especially profit maximization and product sales and design, and to the internal structure of the corporate bureaucracy. Concerning the primary goal of business corporations, Conklin (1977, 41) quotes a corporate executive:

> the goal of a business corporation is to make a profit ... the only goal of a business corporation is to make the maximum possible profit. .... Completely, the only goal of a business corporation is to make the maximum possible profit over a long period of time.

When it was suggested to Alfred P. Sloan, Jr., the president of General

Motors circa 1930, that he should have safety glass installed in Chevrolets, he refused, with the statement, "accidents or no accidents, my concern in this matter is a matter of profit and loss" (quoted in Sherrill 1987, 51). The seemingly ceaseless striving for profits inheres in the mode of production, as does the corresponding pursuit of monetary success. As Clinard (1983, 18) notes, though corporations "may have other goals such as the increase or maintenance of corporate power and prestige, along with corporate growth and stability, their paramount objectives are the maximization of profits and the general financial success of the corporation."

Studies of cover-ups by asbestos companies of cancer-causing hazards (Simon and Eitzen 1986, 112); bribery and corruption by transnational corporations (Fisse and Braithwaite 1983, 144-61); hazards in the workplace (Walters 1985, 60); unsafe pollution control equipment and shoddy products that break and need to be replaced (Clinard 1979, 57); data falsification, unethical sales practices, and the manufacture and marketing of unsafe products in the drug and chemical industries (Carey 1987, 163-69; Clinard 1979, 7; Coleman 1989, 45); high and harmful risks in the nuclear research industry (Faulkner 1987, 170-84); automobile repair frauds (Braithwaite 1978; Farberman 1975); and the dumping of harmful and hazardous products on Third World markets (Mintz 1987, 30-46; Dowie 1987a, 47-580; Simon and Eitzen 1986, 153) demonstrate that large vertical sectors of corporate bureaucracies are involved in the commission of crimes. The pressure of competition, "the most sacred value of capitalist societies, is criminogenic" and once entrenched in the bureaucracy, illegal activities become "part of the structure which sustains the offence" (Snider 1988, 242). Wheeler and Rothman (1982) bluntly state that the corporation is for corporate criminals "what the gun or the knife is for the common criminal — a tool to obtain money from victims." Translated thus, we might conclude that anyone can rob a bank but the most effective way to rob a bank is to own one (Braithwaite 1991, 46).

Ford Motor Company's decision to manufacture and market the Pinto when it knew it was unsafe was clearly motivated by the profit goals of the corporation. Much research has documented that Ford (1) rushed its new subcompact Pinto into production in response to the fear of foreign competition and domination of the U.S. subcompact market; (2) shortened the product-development process from forty-three months to twenty-five months to have the Pinto available for 1971; (3) tooled up for production quickly and only subsequently discovered the design defects, and then reckoned that profits dictated that they should proceed, manufacture and sell the defective cars and (4) conducted a cost-benefit analysis and then continued to make and market the Pinto without introducing safety changes because costs would be prohibitive (Dowie

1977, 20-21). Clearly, the corporation, in multiple departments and at various decision-making levels, conspired to break the law.

Farberman (1975) has referred to pressures in the automotive industry and in other highly concentrated industrial sectors as constituting a "criminogenic market structure." In his study of car manufacturers and their dealerships, he discovered that the high concentration of firms in the industry structures criminal innovations on the part of the dealerships. Because the major manufacturers insist that their dealers sell in high volume at a small per-unit profit, there is a strong pressure to maximize sales and minimize service. Faberman found that one criminal innovation was to compensate for small profit margins through repair overcharges and fraudulent warranty work. The beauty of the arrangement for the corporate executives on the manufacturing side of the automobile industry is that they can distance themselves from the criminal consequences of their own imposed rules on dealers. The result is an absence of responsibility, care and control over repair rackets and dealership frauds. As Clinard notes, one may expect that:

> a corporation is most likely to engage in unlawful conduct when support diminishes for legitimate procedures to be used in reaching the profit goal. Under these conditions, firms may violate... laws and the regulations ... if, by complying, the costs to the corporation are too high.

Consider General Motors' product misrepresentation, when to save production costs it substituted Chevrolet motors for specially advertised "Rocket V-8" engines in more than 87,000 Oldsmobiles. Or consider the case of a citrus company's practice of adulterating orange juice and then marketing it as 100 percent pure; the loss to consumers was $1 million. And again in the pharmaceutical industry, false and misleading product advertising led to consumers being taken for $500 million on worthless health goods and cures (Cullen, Maakestad and Cavender 1987, 6).

Profit maximization is not, of course, the sole organizational goal that affects corporate conduct. Goals regarding the product characteristics — design, quality, style, packaging, advertising, etc. — have a profound impact on corporate organizational behaviour. These product goals are concrete, and they link together organizational actors in the production process who embody a collective vested interest and exert pressure from the top down. As Perrow,(1970, 159) Kramer (1982, 82-83) and Snider (1988, 242) note, product goals engender commitment, loyalty and conformity. Promotions, wage increases, status among peers and feelings of work satisfaction are embodied in organizational strategies in relation to product characteristics.

The Richardson-Merrill pharmaceutical company's commitment to certain product goals concerning MER/29, a cholesterol-reducing drug, seems to have played a major role in its decisions about the manufacture of the drug. The product objectives were clear: (1) to market the drug as quickly as possible and (2) to make it available to the growing number of heart disease sufferers at an affordable price. Because of the pressures exerted to attain these goals, several important safety matters were ignored. Laboratory documents and test results were falsified. Misleading statements about side effects were circulated. Knowledge of harmful effects of the drug — partial blindness, hair loss, scaling rashes — was suppressed. Two years and many hundreds of complaints later, the U.S. Federal Drug Administration withdrew its approval, but not before about 500 MER/29 users developed eye cataracts. Consumer safety was not a product goal for the Richardson-Merrill pharmaceutical company. As the decision in one civil suit action put it:

> responsible corporate officials, at least up to the level of vice-president, had knowledge of the true test results of MER/29 when used on animals, and some or all joined in a policy of nondisclosure of the information to the Food and Drug Administration and the medical profession (Stone 1975, 55).

Similarly, A.H. Robins' commitment to its product goals of creating a "reliable and superior" contraceptive device that was mass marketable and affordable to women resulted in safety negligence. Robins' officials learned — six months before marketing the device nationally — that the Dalkon Shield's multifilament tail had a wicking tendency and could transmit deadly bacteria into the uterus. Their own tests argued for caution and further research and testing. But Robins rushed the Shield into the marketplace, promoting it as safe, reliable, and easily and painlessly administered. During the years the Shield was on the market, A.H. Robins conducted no wicking studies on the string and suppressed information from a quality-control engineer at ChapStik, a manufacturing subsidiary of Robins, who claimed that at least 10,000 Shields carried bacteria. The engineer was overruled by his supervisor, as was a plan to stop the wicking because it was too expensive to implement (an extra five cents per device). In effect, quality control was sacrificed for quick promotion and to save money. Despite the screaming, cursing, suing and dying, A.H. Robins for over a decade, never recalled the device, never sent a warning to doctors about deadly side effects and continues at present, even after losing hundreds of millions of dollars in lawsuits, to argue that the Shield is safe (Mintz 1985, 1987).

McDonnell Douglas' plans for the DC-10 airplane included certain product goals that affected the manufacture of the fuselage, including floors and doors. They contracted out the work to the Convair Aerospace Division of General Dynamics. Two of the most important product goals were (1) to design the cargo doors, like those of the DC-8 and DC-9 aircraft, to operate hydraulically and (2) to guarantee airplane weights to customers. However, in the DC-10, the use of actuators for hydraulic control of doors and thus cabin pressure created a weight saving of 84 pounds per plane. Management decided to use electric actuators and vents but, unlike in the DC-8 and DC-9, these were not designed to gradually open the doors if improperly locked. Between August 1969 and June 1972, when the first cargo door blew off a DC-10, pressure tests, engineering memoranda and about one hundred airline complainants had reported problems in locking the cargo doors. Convair's director of product engineering wrote in 1972 of the DC-10's future accident liability as follows:

> The fundamental safety of the cargo door latching system has been progressively degraded since the program began in 1968. . . . I would expect this to usually result in the loss of the airplane (quoted in Henry 1986, 188).

In March 1974, shortly after takeoff at a Paris airport, a DC-10 crashed. All 334 passengers and twelve crew members were killed. A cargo door had blown off, sudden depressurization had collapsed the floor structure and, because the control cables ran through the floor, control over the plane had been lost. By 1979, McDonnell-Douglas had paid more than $60 million to the families of the people killed (Henry 1986, 188-89). Once again safety as a product goal was secondary to weight guarantees to customers and reduced manufacturing costs. The DC-10 program support manager's recommendation for construction of a safer door was:

> a tacit admission on Convair's part that the original concurrence by Convair on the design philosophy was in error. . . . We have an interesting legal and moral problem, and I feel any direct conversation with Douglas should be based on the assumption that, as a result, Convair may subsequently find itself in a position where it must assume all or a significant part of the costs that are involved (ibid., 189).

Organizational goals are linked to the internal structure of the corporate bureaucracy, to its division of labour, hierarchy of authority, promotion system and value system (Box 1983, 38-42; Kramer 1982, 85; Snider 1988, 242). Two basic functions are served: (1) the regulation of individual conduct and (2) the positioning and exercise of power and authority in decision making.

The internal arrangements of corporate bureaucracy are related to corporate crime in a number of ways. First, as corporations become more complex, they tend to develop an elaborate division of specialized tasks, work teams, departments, territories, geographical divisions, etc. As an example, consider the General Electric Corporation (Clinard and Yeager 1980, 24-25):

> The corporation is like a pyramid. The great majority of the company's workers form the base of the pyramid; they take orders coming down from above but do not give orders to anyone else. If you were hired by GE for one of these lowest level positions, you might find yourself working on an assembly line, installing a motor in a certain type of refrigerator. You would be in a group of five to 50 workers who all take orders from one supervisor, or foreman, or manager. Your supervisor is on the second step of the pyramid; she or he, and the other supervisors who specialize in this type of refrigerator, all take orders from a General Manager.
>
> There are about 180 of these General Managers at GE; each one heads a Department with one or two thousand employees. The General Manager of your Department, and the General Managers of the one or two other Departments which produce GE's other types of refrigerators, are in turn supervised by the Vice President/General Manager of the Refrigerator Division. This man (there are only men at this level and above) is one of the 50 men at GE responsible for heading GE's Divisions. He and the heads of several other Divisions which produce major appliances, look up to the next step of the pyramid and see, towering above, the Vice President/Group Executive who heads the entire Major Appliance Group. While there are over 300,000 workers at the base of the pyramid, there are only 10 men on this Group Executive level. Responsibility for overseeing all of GE's product lines is divided between the ten. At about the same level of authority in the company are the executives of GE's Corporate Staff; these men are concerned not with particular products but with general corporate matters such as accounting, planning, legal affairs, and relations with employees, with the public and with government.

And now the four men at the top of the pyramid come into view; the three Vice Chairmen of the Board of Directors, and standing above them, GE's Chief Executive. . . . Usually, these four men confer alone, but once a month, 15 other men join them for a meeting. The 15 other members of the Board of Directors are not called up from the lower levels of the GE pyramid; they drift in sideways from the heights of neighbouring pyramids. Thirteen of them are chairmen or presidents of other corporations, the fourteenth is a former corporate chairman, and the fifteenth is a university president.

Note the complexity, size, role diversification, and diffusion of decision-making responsibilities. These factors suggest that corporations are autonomous bureaucratic systems within which individuals come and go and within which crimes are easily committed. As Cressey (1976) states:

It is possible that corporation crime, like Cosa Nostra crime, persists because it is "organized," meaning that it is perpetuated by an apparatus rather than by individuals occupying positions in the division of labour constituting the apparatus.

Second, a number of criminologists have argued that the structure of the modern corporation allows a power imbalance to prevail "in which those individuals at the top experience a kind of freedom, while those at the bottom often experience a kind of pressure applied from the top" that encourages and cultivates a wide variety of corporate crimes (Hagan 1987, 329; Kramer 1982, 86). At the top, this arrangement allows for abdication of moral and legal responsibility and fosters a "corporate executive right not to know" what is going on in their own organization. Executive distancing and disengagement from corporate criminality, by all accounts, is increasing, with more and more corporate heads and directors reporting their inability to be honest. Brenner and Molander (1977) reported that nearly 50 percent of subordinates surveyed felt that their superiors did not want to know how results were obtained, as long as the right outcome was realized. Clinard (1979, 7) captures this process very well:

Executives at the higher levels can absolve themselves of responsibility of rationalizing that the operationalization of their broadly stated goals has been carried out, without their knowledge. A sharp split can develop between what the upper levels believe is going on below and the actual procedures being carried out below. There may even be genuine ignorance about the production level. It is also not simply that the lower levels, for whatever reasons, do not wish to inform the higher ups; often, the upper levels do not want to be told.

A fundamental principle of organizational physics, it seems, is that bad news does not flow upstream.

Third, increasingly, pressure from the top down is itself criminogenic. Denzin (1977) on the liquor industry, Dowie (1977) on auto manufacturing, and Cook (1966) and Geis (1978) on the heavy electrical industry have all demonstrated that higher officials create conditions under which their subordinates find it difficult to refuse involvement in illegal activities. Here is how one official described his actions: "There is no doubt that I juggled the books, but I was under order to balance the books no matter what the means" (quoted in Cressey 1953, 63). Similarly in the case of a $2 billion equity fund fraud, Clinard (1979, 15), reports that, "at company direction, one computer specialist created fictitious insurance policies with a value of $430 million, with yearly premiums totalling $5.5 million." The lawyer for A.H. Robins in the Dalkon Shield case reports that immediately after the company lost its first lawsuit, his superiors ordered him to search for and burn documents that indicated any "knowledge [of] and complicity" in wrongdoing or cover-up. The Attorney did not fully comply, but he did destroy incriminating evidence (Mintz 1985).

A study conducted by the American Management Association found that a majority of the 3,000 executives interviewed "felt under pressure to compromise personal standards to meet company goals" (Luthans and Hodgetts 1976, 53-54), and a 1977 survey found that most managers believed that their colleagues would automatically go along with their superiors' directives, including the marketing of off-standard and possibly dangerous products (Madden 1977, 66). Clinard (1983, 95) in later research discovered that 90 percent of executives surveyed felt that pressures to show profits, reduce costs, produce, and meet sales quotas led "to unethical behaviour within a corporation." Finally, Walters (1985, 60) in her study of occupational health and safety representatives, concluded that "experts employed by companies withheld information, lied, distorted their results, or used poor methodologies, in each case serving the interests of their employers." Company doctors were especially criminogenic, ignoring independent medical opinion and complying with corporate strategies designed to control the labour force.

These organizational influences are not for the most part "crime-coercive" but rather are normative because they are known and lead to common choices.

Executives who commit corporate crime are not coerced into it, they do not necessarily have to go along with the advice or instructions of superiors. They are men who rationally weigh up the advantage of conformity to criminal demands or staying on the path of righteousness (Box 1983, 43).

Braithwaite (1984, 322) provides an example of "coaching" in the pharmaceutical industry. If the president says, 'Look, it's your concern to get around this problem the best way you can. I don't want to know how you do it, but just get the job done.' Then the lower level executive will go and bend the rules. For the most part, the chosen path is to go along with criminal demands because this path seems more likely to advance careers, increase organizational trust and guarantee long-term economic success. So the rules of the "capitalist race," to use Bowles and Edwards' (1985) phrase, call for a certain type of cultural personality. Skill and achievement orientation are honed through training classes and socialization processes that attune members to organizational goals. The corporate firm then "must ensure that members' motivations and values are consistent with the organization's needs" (Vaughan 1983, 69).

Thus, corporate lawbreaking is rooted in the norms of the bureaucracy and generally supported by the dominant administrative team of the organization. The new employee at a corporation is not typically socialized into an environment marked by clear ethical sensibilities and discussions of social obligations. Instead, quantifiable performance measures based on sales figures, volume, costs, production output, market shares and quarterly profits pervade the corporate cultural climate. When faced with choices about "bending the rules," "looking the other way" or "making a profit on the side," the new job holder is likely to experience strong pressure "to get on board". As Carey (1978, 384) notes of pharmaceutical executives involved in the manufacturing of unsafe drugs: "No one involved expressed any strong repugnance or even opposition to selling the unsafe drug [an anticholesterol product]. Rather, they all seemed to drift into the activity without thinking a great deal about it."

So, often illegal or unethical practices are "built into" the corporate organization so that they appear to be part of the normal business routine. They are taken for granted and not questioned. One General Electric official convicted for his role in fixing market prices commented that price-setting "had become so common and gone on for so many years that we lost sight of the fact that it was illegal" (quoted in Geis 1978, 123). This suggests that the social psychological consequences of success within a corporation are criminogenic. The top organizational positions require distinctive features which corporate crime also requires: ambition, shrewdness and moral flexibility (Gross 1978; Box 1983).

Corporate executives are often willing personnel in criminal activities because they identify strongly with the goals of the organization as the means to their own personal prosperity (Carey 1978; Cook 1966; Margolis 1979). Gross (1978a, 71) puts it well:

> they will have discovered that their own goals are best pursued through assisting the organization to attain its goals. While this is less true, or even untrue at the bottom of the organization, those at the top share directly in the benefits of the organizational goal achievement, such as seeing their stock go up, deferred compensation, and fringe benefits.

Executives have learned that competition, ambition and organizational pragmatism, and not meekness, passivity and moral forthrightness, enabled them to obtain the "just desserts" of top management. As Waters (1978, 10) observes, "conversations about moral and ethical issues are almost doomed to be awkward, halting and time-consuming to the point of painfulness" and are therefore unlikely to happen. Here is how Lockheed Aircraft Company's special review committee that investigated foreign and domestic illegal payments and practices summed it up:

> Employers learned not to question deviations from standard operating procedures and practices. Moreover, the committee was told by several witnesses that employees who questioned foreign marketing practices damaged their claims for career advancement (Clinard and Yeager 1980, 65).

The lessons are clear: outthink and outwit competitors, seize the opportunity when it arrives, shift with the times and the issues, and don't lose sight of what the organization wants. Gross (1978a, 71) concludes:

> if the organization must engage in illegal activities to attain its goals, men with a non-demanding moral code will have the least compunctions about engaging in such behaviour. . . . they are most likely to believe that they can get away with it without getting caught. Besides they are shrewd.

The situational demands and imperatives of career mobility within a corporate bureaucracy put executives "in a high state of preparedness to commit corporate crime" should they deem it necessary for the good of the company (Box 1983, 41). The rewards for the compliant corporate executive include salaries increased by bonuses based on profits, deferred compensation, consultancy benefits and extensive perks (Clinard and Yeager 1980, 275).

Finally, the extensive, complicated and internally fissured corporate bureaucracy helps participants in corporate crime to shield and protect themselves from the negative consequences of their actions. As Snider (1988, 242) observes of the Lockheed Aircraft Company bribery scandal:

> [it] involved a long list of employees, each of whom was responsible for only one part of the crime. One would get the money ready for delivery; another would put it in an envelope; another would carry the envelope onto the plane; and yet another would deliver it to the recipient. When the illegal act is broken into so many constituent parts ... bribery seems a very different act, and those engaged in it easily disassociate themselves from the consequences of their collective actions.

Similarly, the decisions to manufacture and market defective automobiles, airplanes, pharmaceuticals and contraceptive devices were made in small steps at different levels and times within the corporate hierarchies at Ford, Convair, Richardson-Merrill and A.H. Robins. John DeLorean, recalling his experiences as a former vice-president at General Motors, commented on corporate pressures and the moral indifference of corporate lawbreaking:

> There wasn't a man in top G.M. management who had anything to do with the Corvair who would purposely build a car that he knew would hurt or kill people. But, as part of a management team pushing for increased sales or profits, each gave his individual approval in a group to decisions which produced the car in the face of serious doubts that were raised about its safety, and then later sought to squelch information which might prove the car's deficiencies (quoted in Green and Berry1985, 270-71).

The structures of the corporations separate the decision-makers from the consequences of their actions, and the executives who authorize defective products rarely confront the victims of their corporate decisions. Such "crimaloids," as E.A. Ross (1907, 10-11) called these rich and powerful businessmen, plan their transgressions "leagues or months away from their evil." They hide behind the mantle of corporate anonymity, and their methods are characterized by a smug "indirectness and refinement."

Indeed, the organizational structures of corporations make possible criminal gains on a magnitude that far exceeds the results of individuals acting alone. Wheeler and Rothman (1982) note that the median "take" for corporate organizational offenders ($117,392) was about thirty times the "take" for individual offenders ($5,279). By deploying the resources of the corporation, they are able to commit crimes that involve larger numbers of victims spread over larger territories. They perpetuate what Hagan (1987, 329) calls "bigger and better crimes" and confirm the wisdom of Merton's (1957) notion of organizational "innovation." As Finney and Lesieur (1982, 289) note, "organizations ... commit crimes to achieve their objectives and solve their problems, and that commitment to deviant courses of action involves normal processes of decision making under conditions of limited rationality."

The criminogenic character of the modern corporation — its opportunities, goals, and motivations — are bolstered further by ideological supports that provide a litany of verbal neutralizations of law and rationalizations for illegal corporate behaviour. To start, the corporation itself is a "legal fiction" with "no pants to kick or soul to damn" (Stone 1975, 3). Since they are treated as "juristic persons," liable to the same law as natural persons, corporations cannot be incarcerated or face death. More importantly, it is difficult to ascribe specific corporate responsibility and conscience (Marchak 1979). As Stone (1975, 35) notes, "if we decide to look beyond the individual employees and find an organizational 'mind' to work with, a 'corporate conscience' distinct from individuals," we discover it is ambiguous and amorphous. Corporate power is unchecked and, as we shall see in the next chapter, much too little is expected from corporations in the way of legal control over their individual employees.

The ideological significance of the guilty corporate conscience, however, is profound. It is an obstacle to imposing corporate liability, and it leads to a legal double standard. Thus Justice Dickson of the Supreme Court of Canada writes that "true crimes" are expressed in the "doctrine of the guilty mind expressed in terms of intention or recklessness but not negligence." Regulatory or public welfare offenses "are not criminal in any real sense, but are prohibited in the public interest." So defined, they are "in substance of a civil nature and might well be regarded as a branch of administrative law to which traditional principles of criminal law have but limited application" (quoted in Sargent 1990, 107). Yet everyday enforcement of regulatory offenses such as pollution, workplace safety, and consumer health and protection are frequently managed under the Criminal Code even though they are said to constitute a special realm of regulation. Falling betwixt and between, corporate offenses are thus relatively immune from criminal sanctions despite harm caused and culpability exhibited (Sargent 1989, 53).

According to Box (1983, 54); Clinard and Yeager (1980, 69-73); Coleman (1989, 211-17); and Hills (1987, 190), the absence of legal clarity and control is compounded further by the fact that corporate officials operate in a bureaucratic world of "pragmatic amorality and ethical numbness" that enables, empowers and justifies corporate lawbreaking without too many pangs of conscience. Following Matza (1969), Box (1983, 54) argues that structural immoralities are particularly important in neutralizing the moral bond of law because corporate officials are "comparatively more committed to conventional values and a respectable self-identity" than typical lower-class adolescents and adults. The corporate environment provides precepts, and customs, norms and sentiments that posit certain beliefs, which together function as the legitimate extenuating conditions under which crime is allowable (Snider 1988, 242-43; Hills 1987). As Coleman (1989, 211-12) notes, these "techniques of neutralization are not just ex posto facto rationalization, they ... form part of the motivation for the original act." Thus corporate criminals are aware of their crimes, and rationalizations make it psychologically feasible for them to carry them out.

What are the common methods of neutralization? How is ethical numbness created? First, corporate personnel can deny responsibility for their actions, and do so by pleading ignorance, accident or that they were just following orders. They often interpret legal regulations as vague, inconsistent, ambiguous and confusing: "The law really isn't clear so we didn't know we were violating it." The president of Reed Paper Limited, for example, argued that mercury poisoning was not harmful and certainly not illegal. The corporation, he said, had in effect a "license to pollute" from the Ontario government. "I think there are many instances in our society where people are harmed ... through no fault of their own, and it's particularly difficult when blame is not exclusive ... you almost have to define [blame] in the courts, split up where is the responsibility ... I don't know exactly what we've done. Nobody has told us what the consequences of our actions were" (quoted in Shkilnyk 1985, 190). As Conklin (1977, 92) observes, "many businessmen who violate the law are aware that they are taking a risk. ... They test the limits of the law and try to keep, just inside an imaginary boundary thought to separate the condoned from the condemned."

Claiming that a crime was an "accident" is a technique to deny intent and responsibility: "I did not want to hurt anyone, I just did it for the good of the company." Thus the consequences, in retrospect, may be unhappy, but they are viewed as irrelevant and accidental when establishing criminal intent and liability. To argue, "How could corporate officials have committed a crime if they did not know it was a crime in the first place?" is a powerful rhetorical means to negate an already diminished sense of corporate conscience (Clinard and Yeager 1980, 70-72; Hills 1987). A defendant in a corruption case said, "I will never believe I have done anything inimically wrong. I did what is business. If I bent any rules, who doesn't? If you are going to punish me, sweep away the system" (Chibnall and Saunders 1977, 142). Rationalizations such as these are systematized and transmitted as generalizations in the business bureaucracy by phrases such as "we are not in business for our health," "business is business," or "no business was ever built on the beatitudes" (Sutherland 1961, 240).

Another way to avoid responsibility is to shift the blame onto others, usually higher officials. "I was told to do it. The company wanted it done that way. I was just following orders. I did not even think about it as a crime." This is achieved by reducing and subordinating oneself, the individual employee, into a clone of the organizational "mind" (Stone 1975). Here is how one co-conspirator in the B.F. Goodrich aerospace fraud case put it after being asked to go along with the manufacture of false data:

> Well it looks like we're licked. The way it stands now, we're to go ahead and prepare the data and other things for the graphic presentation in the report, and when we're finished, someone upstairs will actually write the report... we're just drawing some curves, and what happens to them after they leave here, well, we're not responsible for that (Vandivier,1978, 90).

Another supervisor, when challenged by a lab technician to report a cover-up of "fudged" test data, refused and replied, "It's none of my business, and it's none of yours. I learned a long time ago not to worry about things over which I had no control. I have no control over this. . . . why should my conscience bother me?" (ibid.).

A second method of neutralization that acts to limit the harm and cost of corporate criminal behaviour is to deny the victim (Box 1983, 55; Clinard and Yeager 1980, 72; Hills 1987a, 197-98; Coleman 1989, 213). When the subject of harm is a tax department, a corporate competitor, an insurance company or, as in the case of price-fixing in the Canadian petroleum industry, millions of consumers deprived of small amounts of money, or when entire nations are abused as in the case of transnational corporate bribery and corruption, then it is possible for corporate officials to come to the conclusion that "no real pain occurred, no real person is suffering." Thus, Geis (1978, 68) reports what one corporate conspirator in a price-fixing case said:

> There was not an attempt to actually damage customers, charge excessive prices, there was no personal gain in it for me, the company did not seem actually to be defrauding. . . . So I guess morally it did not seem quite so bad.

Similarly, corporate officials in the automobile industry often insist that their cars are safe, but that road conditions and incompetent drivers are the problem.

> Automotive "safety engineers" . . . will advocate spending billions educating youngsters, punishing drunks and redesigning street signs. Listening to them, you can momentarily begin to think that it is easier to control 100 million drivers than a handful of manufacturers. They show movies about guardrail design and advocate the clear-cutting of trees 100 feet back from every highway in the nation. If a car is unsafe, they argue, it is because its owner doesn't drive properly. Or, perhaps, maintain it (Hills 1987, 197).

This is a very convenient and persuasive ideological construction since it distances and reconstructs the persons who are harmed, robbed and sometimes killed from the actions of the corporate violators and reconstructs them as "non-persons" (Goffman 1964). Nowhere is this process more pernicious than among companies employing agricultural workers in Central American countries, where almost anything becomes permissible: pesticide poisoning, dangerous drugs, dumping carcinogenic garments and banned products, unprotected and unregulated workplaces and work procedures, and severe wage exploitation (Frank 1985).

> The people who work in the fields are treated like half humans. . . . when an airplane flies over to spray, they can leave if they want, but they won't be paid their seven cents a day, or whatever. They often live in huts in the middle of the fields. Their homes, their children and their food get contaminated (quoted in Hills 1987, 198).

A third technique whereby corporate officials are able to transform opportunities and motives into actual criminal behaviours while at the same time denying their guilt is to place themselves above the law and condemn the condemners. The law is said to be "unworkable," "undesirable," "unnecessary," "unfair" and "hypocritical." Either because legislation is restrictive of capital accumulation or because the government is thought to be incompetent or duplicitous, corporate executives can argue to themselves that the rule of law should be disregarded or circumvented and the state condemned as intrusive (Clinard and Yeager 1980, 69-72: Coleman 1989, 213-14; Hills 1987). Consider again the case of the electrical conspiracy where corporate executives divided markets and fixed prices in clear defiance of the U.S. Sherman Antitrust Act. Officials knew they were breaking the law. They used pay phones, plain paper, home addresses and assumed names in their communications about price-rigging. The list of names for meetings was known as the "Christmas Card List" and price-fixing meetings were called "choir practice" (Geis 1978, 65). The testimony of a Westinghouse executive is illustrative:

> Committee Attorney: Did you know that these meetings with competitors were illegal?
> Witness: Illegal? Yes, but not criminal. I didn't find that out until I read the indictment. . . . I assumed that criminal action meant damaging someone, and we did not do that. . . I thought that we were more or less working on a survival basis in order to try to make enough to keep our plant and our employees (ibid., 67).

The president and general-manager of Allen-Bradley Company, also charged in the electrical conspiracy, explained his behaviour as follows:

> No one attending the gathering was so stupid he didn't know the meetings were in violation of the law. But it is the only way a business can be run. It is free enterprise (Henry 1986, 193).

In 1985 a chemical leak at the Union Carbide plant in West Virginia hospitalized 135 workers. The Occupational Safety and Health Administration (OSHA) investigated and imposed a $1.4 million fine on the corporation for over two hundred violations of fifty-five federal safety and health laws. The angry response of the company president was to condemn the regulatory agency as "being on their back." The OSHA, he said, grossly distorted the actual safety conditions of the plant. Most of the citations, he said, were entirely unjustified (Hills 1987, 199).

Finally, corporate officials commonly resort to appeals to higher values and authorities to promote and excuse their corporate criminality. Profits, the moral superiority of the corporation, business ethics, the free enterprise system, and the values of "our way of life," "the family," "our country" have all at various times been deployed by corporate executives to mark differences between economic morality and formal law, and to claim their allegiance for the former over the latter (Box 1983; Coleman 1989, 214-15). Silk and Vogel (1976, 228) found that top executives violated the law for reasons of economic survival because "if they did not, their stockholders would suffer, and other firms 'with less scrupulous management' would win out." They identify with and appeal to a higher loyalty than law and order and thereby free themselves from its moral restriction. As Clinard and Yeager (1980, 68) note:

> The diverse defenses continually offered by corporations ... to explain corporate violations of law serve to justify illegal activity in a society that professes law obedience to be one of its highest ideals.

Whether because corporate executives are insulated in an occupational subculture or because they are driven by the profit goal, they seem able to break the law without feeling guilt or tarnishing their self-respect. Consider the following comment by a high-ranking official of a distilling company: "We break the laws every day. If you think I go to bed at night worrying about it, you're crazy. Everybody breaks the law" (quoted in Denzin 1977, 919). Another official justified unsafe health conditions in an asbestos plant by arguing that saving jobs is more important than obeying the law. "I think we are all willing to have a little bit of crud in our lungs and a full stomach," he said, "rather than a whole lot of clean air and nothing to eat" (quoted in Michalowski 1985, 334). Convicted politician Michel Gravel, who committed fraud and took bribes on Canadian government contracts, claimed that what he did was not really illegal. "I thought it was politics," he stated (*Globe and Mail*, June 22, 1991). Illegalities are seen as indispensable to doing business and, taken to the extreme, the erosion of norms of propriety can become "so extensive within an organization that unlawful conduct occurs regardless of resource scarcity" (Vaughan 1983, 61). Indeed, conspiring to commit corporate crimes may become a way of life in some industries. In the words of one executive indicted in a price-fixing arrangement in the paper industry, "It's always been done in this business, and there's no real way of ever being able to stop it — not through Congress, not the Justice Department. It may slow for a few years. But it will always be there." (Clinard and Yeager 1980, 141).

This final piece of identity management is furthered by the official portrait of crime as being essentially a lower class activity. Box (1983, 57) observes:

Since murder, assault, and theft are committed by working class men, corporate executives see their own virtue reflected in the guilt of those beneath them. Thus corporate officials are both mystified as to their own crime, and misdirected as to the distribution of crime in general. Both mystification and misdirection preserve the appearance of corporate respectability and help keep invisible to themselves and others the underlying ugly reality of corporate crime.

Ironically, however, this ideological construction — that the rich get richer and the poor get prison — may provide other social groups with a persuasive justification for their own forms of criminality. As the editor of *Fortune* magazine mused, "How much crime in the streets is connected with the widespread judgement that the business economy itself is a gigantic rip-off?" (quoted in Stone 1975, xi). Corporate mystification about crime may cause profound damage to other social relations and to the corporate world's own claims to moral legitimacy. This is a point I will develop in Chapter 5.

Corporate crime is structured by capital accumulation, bureaucracy, and a subculture of ethical numbness and immorality, but it is also important to recognize that it is a gendered criminal enterprise. Most corporate crimes, like most conventional crimes and especially violent crimes, are committed by men. Of course, one could say that this is because women do not occupy the key offices of corporate power. And it is true that they have been explicitly and implicitly excluded from official power positions for a long time. But even so, corporate offenders are almost always men. Why? Is corporate criminality connected to masculinity? Is there an elective affinity between the rules of profits first, bureaucratic reasoning and male character structure? Do we need to understand corporate crime as a gender-specific form of criminal conduct?

We have seen that while corporate executives are working, they are not just producing products and profits. They are also producing culture. The relations that surround the corporate suite are made up of the things people do and the things they believe and say. We also have seen how profits, economic rationality, authority and hierarchy, and ideology come together to facilitate and reproduce corporate crime. But the world of the corporate boardroom is truly a public assembly of men. Though women appear to have greater access to occupations and professions that have been regarded as the province of men, it is men, nevertheless, who police access and entry into careers and who continue to fill the top positions in industry. Benjamin (1988, 187) notes:

> Thus, regardless of woman's increasing participation in the public, productive sphere of society, it remains, in its practices and principles, "a man's world." The presence of women has no effect on its rules and processes.

Men have appropriated the business and technological sphere. They have valourized certain attitudes and types of knowledge and disqualified others. Cockburn (1985), in her study of engineering firms, shows how corporate executives made use of a "hard/soft" dichotomy to appropriate challenging, physical engineering work for men and to associate masculinity with rationality and intellect. Femininity, in contrast, was seen as linked to irrationality and the absence of strength and conviction. Here is one of her engineering executives talking:

> "You've got to be (sigh), a very hard person. . . . You've got to be tough. . . . You've got to take the knocks, a lot of cuts. . . . I don't know that a woman would have the same attitude. I know we're built differently, physically. . . . you've got to be courageous (ibid., 192).

Women are often portrayed as inauthentic workers, unsuitable for corporate power because supposedly they are not achievement-oriented and are passive, private and emotional people. Here is how one executive put it:

> There are hardly any female general managers in my industry. Either because of family commitments or because they don't think they can do it and aren't pushy enough. . . . I don't think women have the confidence (ibid., 185-86).

Collinson and Collinson (1989), in their study of insurance and engineering industries, reveal how the domination of men's assumptions and practices with regard to sexuality have been reflected and reproduced in the male-dominated character of corporate organization, resulting in demeaning, discrediting and excluding behaviour towards women that is sanctioned by corporate management. DiTomaso (1989) reports that in manufacturing, service and public firms, women faced particularly aggressive forms of sexual harrassment and discrimination, especially where they competed for "male jobs" or otherwise challenged male authority in the organization. Sheppard (1989), in her survey of women managers, shows how women were either coerced to enter the male culture of the corporation on stereotypical terms or forced to devise elaborate gender management strategies involving deliberate techniques of dressing, speaking and acting aimed at desexualizing themselves and their organizational relations. Organizational sexuality was overtly male and was "used as a means of asserting prevailing organizational power relations and definitions by reducing women to a devalued organizational status" (ibid., 156).

The culture of corporate organization often signals to women that they are not regarded as full members: access is restricted to corporate networks, especially those rooted in male-centred leisure activities; organizational power often depends upon involvement in officially sanctioned but male-oriented social activities; the availability of sponsors and mentors is largely confined to males; the motivating language of the corporation is frequently expressed in male-oriented metaphors; and the politics of sexuality overtly and covertly discriminates against women (Gutek 1989; Collinson and Collinson 1989; Pringle 1989). As Ferguson (1984) notes, even where the inclusion of women in the corporation is preferred, the bureaucratic form of discourse, which favours men, creates cultural barriers to women's performance and success. Women have enormous obstacles to overcome in a corporate world view that reflects male thought and styles of communication.

The social world of corporate power is in reality a gendered discourse, one in which a particular type of masculinist ethos is predominant. This does not mean that all men accept or live by the code or that some women do not abide by it as well. Masculinity and femininity are not, as Segal (1987, 1990), Brittan (1989) and Benjamin (1988) have shown, single and simple homogenous states but, rather, complex, contradictory and changing social statuses. Segal (1990) speaks of "competing masculinities," and Brittan (1989, 1) cautions that "masculinity" is not universal or innate, but a cultural and historically specific social construction. In his words, "We cannot talk of masculinity, only masculinities." But it must also be said that there is a dominant form of masculinity. Corporate power and organizations have produced a specific kind of male personality structure that appears "receptive to the exigencies of competitive stress in the marketplace" (ibid.). This image appears in the various forms of power men ideally possess: the power to assert control over women, over other men, over their own bodies, over machines and technology (Cockburn 1985). In the business world the masculine ideal is the tough-as-nails man who has a predisposition towards authoritarian competitiveness and aggression, power, dominance and submission, manipulation and rationality, and who withholds caring, nurturing, sympathetic and emotional responses (Tolson 1977). In Gilligan's (1982) view, the corporate world ignores a conception of rationality and morality concerned with responsibility and care and favours a mode of ethical judgement deemed to be unemotional, impersonal, competitive, objective and inexorable. According to her, modern institutions, including law and politics, have become imbricated with male-centred modes of reasoning, and this has resulted in an undervaluation and repression of feminine moral thinking with its emphasis on feelings and the maintenance of responsibility and relationships in the resolution of public moral and legal dilemmas. Similarly, Benjamin (1988, 186) has noted that corporate power is located in the principle of commodity exchange and in the system of bureaucratic administration but, for her, "the instrumental orientation and the impersonality that govern modern social organization" are not universal. She argues that bureaucracy, with its means and ends thinking, is masculine in character. And Segal (1990, 130), concludes that contemporary masculinity is deeply rooted in the system of production and is now primarily a matter of "mind rather than muscle, manipulation rather than endurance." The corporate work world is a major site where competitive masculinity is created and reproduced.

Gender is one of our tools for thinking, ordering, understanding and acting in the public world. Lloyd (1984, 37) has explored the way "Reason," the philosophical concept that underlies technology, corporate behaviour and science, is itself gendered. The "Man of Reason," she says, was conceived as "transcending the feminine," and so women were not usually viewed as possessing or sharing in rationality. Women were not simply excluded as persons from the business world, Lloyd stresses, but the very construction of reason viewed women and the feminine as unreason and so as unwanted in the corporate boardroom and in the halls of law, science and medicine. She argues that basic assumptions and ideas were themselves fundamentally genderized and in the process came to discriminate against the presence of women in public life and against a feminine form of moral reasoning that is contextual, concrete and views the self in relation to others and their social and moral problems. Similarly, Merchant (1980) argues that the critical economic, technological and scientific changes of the seventeenth century shattered the organic community in which men and women lived in relative harmony with nature and themselves. For Merchant, instrumental rationality consolidated male power over women. A new cognitive and moral order emerged that devalued nature and women. She notes:

> Between 1500 and 1700 an incredible transformation took place.
> . . . A subsistence economy in which goods, money, or labour
> were exchanged for commodities was replaced in many areas by
> the open-ended accumulation of profits in an international mar-

ket. Living animate nature died, while dead inanimate money
was endowed with life. Increasingly, capital and the market
would assume the organic attributes of growth, strength, activity, pregnancy, weakness, decay, and collapse, obscuring and
mystifying the new underlying social relations of production
and reproduction.... Nature, women, blacks and wage labourers
were set on a path as "natural" and human resources for the
modern world system. Perhaps the ultimate irony in these trans-
formations was the name given them: rationality (ibid., 288).

In Merchant's view, rationality was not and is not gender neutral.
Rather it was imbued with masculinist assumptions, logic and moral
thinking that in effect disadvantaged the female sex historically and
continues to do so to the present day. Keller (1985), in another context,
makes an equally convincing argument for the gender bias of modern
scientific reasoning. By exploring the emergence and development of
science, she shows how gender came to frame the relationship between
mind and nature. The impersonality and detachment of modern science
from the object of study, Keller argues, is actually the sign of its male
identity. The all-controlling and dominant subject of science stresses
autonomy, separation and opposition. The world outside, the other, is
always object and something to be conquered. In the radical separation
of subject and object, we perceive again, she says, the male posture of one-
sided differentiation that finds difficulty in appreciating the significance
of the other and in caring, merging and identifying with the other.

Rationality, so constructed, rejects the commonality between mind
and nature and does not allow attunement, communion and familiarity
between knower and known. It leads to an instrumental and abstract
mode of problem solving in the public corporate world, which favours
contestation, mastery, deceit, force and domination over nurturance and
empathy. Thus, the public world of men is more likely to espouse a
formalized and detached "ethic of justice" that operates with a principle
of reciprocity in the abstract — the universal generalized other — and yet
disqualifies the specific, discrete, contextual and individual (Gilligan
1982). The logic of gender polarity may thus be expressed as follows:
competition/economic success = public = men; nurturance/responsibil-
ity = private = women. But this form of public rationality necessitates that
the feminine ethos and voice be split off and institutionalized in the
private sphere, in the family and in the home. Nurturance and rationality
are thus dichotomized in social life, and the public world of corporate
bureaucracy is "conceived as a place in which direct recognition and care
for others' needs is impossible" or at best unlikely (Benjamin 1988, 197).

The public world of corporate bureaucracy is thus a reflection of male power and of a type of male moral reasoning. It exists as a separate sphere through the combined hegemony of (1) impersonal organization, (2) formal rules that refer to the supposed interaction of autonomous individuals, (3) instrumental knowledge predicated in the subject's calculated control of the "exterior" world, and (4) the pursuit of profit which bows to neither need nor tradition. And this protean impersonality, this apparent neutrality and objectivity, this seemingly fair and just viewpoint hides its real gender authorship and identity. Benjamin (1988, 187) notes:

> The public institutions and the relations of production display an apparent genderlessness, so impersonal do they seem. Yet it is precisely this objective character, with its indifference to personal need, that is recognized as the hallmark of masculine power. It is precisely the pervasive depersonalization, the banishment of nurturance to the private sphere, that reveals the logic of male dominance.

To put it bluntly, masculinity lurks behind gender-neutrality. Nowhere is this more obvious than in the corporate boss-secretary relationship with its master-slave discourse. Corporate executives can decide for themselves to what extent they will keep family and work, their public and private lives, separate. Secretaries do not have this luxury. Male executives and managers enter their secretaryies' offices unannounced, assume the right to comment on their looks, clothes and language, and intrude on their non-work lives by having them do personal chores, by surveying their families, friends and future plans, by phoning them at home and by expecting them to do overtime at a moment's notice (Pringle 1989, 169). Secretaries rarely have such power. Men, in this case, "invade" women's private space, blurring the division between home and work but almost always doing so on terms they control. Even where one finds nurturance and empathy in the corporate world, it is not where the power resides but located at a lower and more disqualified level within the organizational structure.

Taken together, these studies strongly suggest that the hallmark of modern corporate bureaucratic organization is a type of heartless masculinist rationality that undervalues collective nurturance and responsibility. Nowhere is this more obvious than in the world of transnational and national corporate crime. As we have seen, the ascendancy of male rationality embodied in bureaucratic reasoning has supplied powerful motives and excuses for corporate crime. It is a cold and abstract calculus, indeed, that underlies the homicides and injuries to workers on the job and to consumers in their homes and neighbourhoods, that damages and degrades the environment, destroys entire communities and defrauds the public and the polity while simultaneously claiming innocence, reasonableness and superiority in such economic conduct.

This framework of gender polarity, especially the public/private split, has largely worked to women's detriment, but it has also fostered and contributed to a public corporate culture of dishonesty in which substantive values are no longer collectively shared or promoted. Dispatched to the periphery of organizational life are many of the most basic positive social attributes: sensitivity to oneself and others, tenderness, respect and empathy, compassionate acknowledgement of fear and weakness, honesty and patience.

Profits, bureaucracy and patriarchy have combined to produce a phallic culture of order and authority in the corporation. Promoted at the core of organizational life is a "play to win at any cost" philosophy and an "end justifies the means" politics. Not surprisingly, the result is a cool, authoritarian, coercive, insensitive masculinity, silencing opposition and discouraging all but the most aggressive and competitive from engaging and succeeding in business. What is not surprising is that this masculinist ethos easily lends support to law evasion, law avoidance and lawbreaking. Against a backdrop of instrumental rationality and a dichotomized social world, corporate men stride and stumble into their illegal and criminal enterprises, loudly proclaiming their virtue and respectability from the bureaucratic shadows in the name of profits.

• 4 •
The Law, the State and
the Control of Corporate Crime

So far, I have argued that corporate motives, structure, personnel, beliefs and masculinist discourse combine to initiate, foster and execute crimes for the good of the corporation. I have stressed that the underlying dynamic of the modern corporation is capital accumulation and profit maximization. But what stands in the way of corporate crime? What does the law do to halt and correct the potential for abuse? What social censures face corporate violators? What limits are there on the structural opportunities to commit crime? These questions raise the issues of legal liability, the power to criminalize behaviour (or not), through apprehension, enforcement, deterrence, and sanction and social censure.

Modern corporations have arranged things, writes Stone (1975, 46), "so that the people who call the shots do not have to bear the full risks." This, in fact, is the consequence of the limited liabilities affecting corporate actors. Six points need to be stressed.

First, Canadian, American and British criminal law rests heavily on the idea that *mens rea*, a "guilty mind," or criminal intent, is a crucial component of culpability. As we have seen, discovering the corporate "mind" or "conscience" is very difficult, if not impossible. For example, in Texas, where corporate criminal liability has been codified, appellate courts still hold that corporations may not be considered liable for homicide because "they are incapable of forming and acting with intent, knowledge or recklessness." (Cullen, Maakestad, Cavender 1987, 325). As a result, the prosecution often focuses on individual executives, managers, and professionals involved in activities such as price-fixing, restraint of trade, marketing unsafe products, bribery or environmental pollution to find the "guilty" party (Hagan 1987, 325-26).

In Canada, not until 1941 was a corporation held criminally liable for an offense requiring proof of *mens rea*. Prior to this time, corporations were immune to criminal liability because legally a corporation could have no guilty mind of its own. Since then, as the *Sault St. Marie* (1978), the *Canadian Dredge and Dock Co. Ltd.* (1985) and the *Southam Inc.* v. *Hunter* (1983) cases heard before the Supreme Court of Canada evince, the courts and legislators have tried to fit corporate offenders into an individualist model of liability, evidence, procedure and sanctioning. This has resulted in some modest progress in that it is now possible for the Crown to obtain criminal convictions against corporations in Canada. A "halfway house" approach now exists where corporations, depending on the *actus reus* (the criminal "act") and on the directions in the enabling legislation, may be charged with offenses that require only strict liability. There is no necessity for the Crown to prove the existence of *mens rea*. However, corporations may avoid liability by proving that they took all reasonable care and showed due diligence. This had made it more possible for the Crown to obtain criminal convictions against corporate offenders. These modest improvements are now in question and the application of absolute liability and strict liability may be eroded because they may violate certain *Canadian Charter of Rights and Freedoms* guarantees claimed by defendant corporations.

The crux of the matter is whether the Charter is meant to extend its protection to corporations as legal persons. Maybe yes, maybe no. The following recent cases — R. v. *Westfair Foods Ltd.* (1986; Manitoba Court of Queen's Bench reports), R. v. *Cancoil Thermal Corporation* (1986; Supreme Court of Ontario reports), R. v. *Multitech Warehouse* (1989; Supreme Court of Ontario reports), R. v. *Wholesale Travel Group Inc.* (1990; Supreme Court of Ontario reports) and R. v. *Nova Scotia Pharmaceutical Society* (1991; Supreme Court of Nova Scotia reports) — all suggest that the answer is in the affirmative. These court decisions have ruled that the Charter does have profound impact on substantive regulatory and criminal laws. In the specific case of corporations, they have tended to restore *mens rea* requirements, in line with the principle of fundamental justice, affirmed protection to corporations under S.7 and S.1(d) of the Charter, and greatly reduced the sting of penalty by ruling that absolute liability offenses for corporations cannot be combined with imprisonment.

However, in the *Irwin Toy Ltd.* case, the Supreme Court of Canada (1989, 1001-4) has ruled that "a corporation cannot avail itself of the protection offered by S.7 of the Charter." Because corporations may not be deprived of their "life, liberty or security of the person" in that it is nonsense to talk of corporations being imprisoned, and because a corporation's economic rights are not constitutionally protected in S.7 of the Charter, the Supreme Court of Canada (1989, 1004) ruled that:

> A plain, common sense reading of the phrase, "Everyone has the right to life, liberty and security of the person" serves to underline the human element involved; only human beings can enjoy these rights.

"Everyone" thus does not apply to corporations. It includes only human beings.

So the matter is confused, and these issues will no doubt be raised before the Canadian Supreme Court. Nevertheless, as Sargent (1989, 55) observes, "Canadian Courts have remained reluctant to extend the scope of corporate criminal responsibility to include the illegal acts or omissions of a corporation's agents or employees, on the basis that vicarious liability has no place in a system of criminal law based on principles of individual responsibility." Equally significant, the more anonymous and complex the corporate criminal actor and the more complex the causal link between the illegal conduct and the harm caused, the less likely "the corporate actor and its human agents will be held criminally responsible or treated with severity by the criminal justice system" (ibid.). The corporation itself remains relatively shielded from legal control.

Second, since most corporate crime is the cumulative result of collective decisions or non-decisions made by a variety of individuals at different times and in different contexts, it is often difficult to determine individual guilt. The complexity of corporate violations, the technical difficulties of using specialized accounting or extensive and expensive laboratory testing to determine truth or falsehood, and the limited rules of evidence that prohibit an extensive search and seizure in order to prove corporate conspiracy or cover-up combine to minimize even individual prosecution (Michalowski 1985, 354-55). Consider the difficulties of establishing guilt in a transnational corporate corruption case:

> In order to obtain judicially admissible evidence, U.S. investigators would have to obtain proof that (1) a payment was intended for a foreign official, (2) it was made with a corrupt intent, and (3) it was made for a prohibited purpose. Collecting such evidence would necessitate the co-operation of foreign governments. Whether foreign governments would allow U.S. investigators to implicate one of their own nationals *under* U.S. *law* is doubtful. .

.. Moreover, a U.S. citizen accused of foreign bribery would be denied due process of law under the U.S. constitution unless he could produce foreign witnesses and documents in his own defence. These essential components of a fair defence would not be available to a defendant, as they are beyond the compulsory judicial process of U.S. federal courts (Braithwaite 1979, 131).

The legal problems for lawyers who wish to prove burden of guilt are almost insurmountable. Even where individual responsibility can be proved, there is no guarantee that the individual will bear the brunt of the judgement. As Stone (1978, 331) notes, "typically, a corporation covers directors and officers with legal liability insurance or indemnifies them against fines and judgements by, for example, reimbursing them with stockholders' money."

Third, since much crime is carried out by middle-level and lower-level officials, and not directly by upper-level executives, the corporation itself can often deny responsibility or knowledge and hence avoid the burden of prosecution or sanction (Clinard 1983). Transnational corruption is again illustrative.

Many bribes are passed by local agents who act for transnational corporations, rather than by the transnationals themselves. Executives of the transnational clearly know what is going on and allow amounts for their agents' fees appropriate to cover the scale of bribery required to effect a particular company goal. However, a requirement that a transnational be accountable for the way its agents spend their fees would involve a departure from the settled doctrine of common law that a principal is not criminally responsible for the acts of his agent (Braithwaite 1979, 131).

This means that national laws often are often impotent in dealing with transnational crime. No legal order seems able to untangle the complex, interlocking web of responsibility and guilt.

Fourth, given that, in most large corporations, shareholder and management interests are separated and corporate officials gain their primary rewards through salaries, the effects of damage judgements when they do occur are indirect and limited. It would seem that salaries, promotions and other economic benefits such as consultancy fees often follow in the wake of corporate culpability (Stone 1975; Vandivier 1978; Coleman 1989). For example, the chief executive officer of Technical Tape Corporation continued to collect his pay cheque of $125,000 and bonuses of $325,000 while serving a one-year prison sentence for eleven criminal violations of securities laws (Clinard and Yeager 1980, 296). There is little evidence of shareholders successfully changing such patterns by the installation of new management in the wake of lawsuits.

Fifth, criminal laws against corporate behaviour focus almost entirely on the regulations broken and not on the consequences of the action. Frequently corporations are not charged for deaths or injuries caused by their actions or negligence; rather they are prosecuted for not properly maintaining or inspecting equipment or machinery. The fact that employees have died often does not lead to prosecution for that consequence. According to Box (1983, 59), this fracture between violation and consequence does not exist in conventional crime, and it facilitates corporate crime by encouraging irresponsibility and the likelihood of little and lenient punishment.

Finally, most laws against corporate criminal behaviour require that intention be proved before guilt can be ascertained. But intention is very difficult to prove in cases of injury and death to employees, consumers and the public, and in cases of fraud, securities irregularities and other financial crimes there is always the plea that no intention to defraud shareholders existed despite obvious negative consequences such as misappropriation of investment funds, stocks and bonds (Shapiro 1984, 135-66). Corporations as criminal defendants thus tend to enjoy nearly the same constitutional protections as individual citizens. This places a special burden upon prosecuting attorneys who must cope with the fact that corporations can rely on the same due process protections that more traditional defendants invoke. Ironically, protections that were put in place to safeguard the weak and the powerless from a strong state are now being used to excuse corporate wrongdoing. Braithwaite (1984, 339) argues succinctly:

> The tendency automatically to attribute traditional rights and due process protections to corporations simply because they are available to individuals is legal anthropomorphism at its worst. Corporations cannot have a confession physically coerced out of them. . . . Corporations do not stand in the dock without benefit of legal counsel. When corporations do suffer at the hands of the state, the suffering is diffused among many corporate actors — shareholders, managers, workers. The extreme privations suffered by individual victims of state oppression which justify protection of individual rights are not felt within the corporation.

Indeed, the burden-of-proof difficulty is compounded further by vaguely worded laws that are difficult to enforce. Snider (1988, 262-63) lists a few in the Canadian context:

> the Hazardous Products Acts which allow the state to act only after the product is on the market (and after the damage is done); the Food and Drug Act which accepts tests done by the manufacturers as proof that the products are safe; the Occupational Health and Safety Acts which insist on safe working conditions only if they will not affect the financial health of the company.

Important as the above arguments are for explaining why corporate crime is endemic and enduring, the greatest opportunity lies in the power of corporations "to prevent their actions from becoming subject to criminal sanctions in the first place" (Box 1983, 59). Consider the following historical examples (Bliss 1974, 56-59).

- In 1909 mine operators commented that most accidents are not the result of unsafe working conditions or failure to enforce safety rules. "The miner, as a rule, is naturally negligent."
- Railway executives argued that coupling freight cars by hand and running along their tops to apply brakes could be hazardous but not if the men "are looking where they are going. . . . I claim . . . the railway companies are not to blame for injuries or deaths."
- Factory owners routinely disciplined their labour forces. Young apprentices were especially liable to corporal punishment. The use of special constables, the 'black hole' in factory cellars, as well as beatings and degradations were common but necessary because "the young were lazy," "apt to steal," "unruly," and needed to be "chastised" and "corrected."
- Corporate officials repeated again and again that machinery is not in itself dangerous. The workingmen's welfare is their own responsibility. Their own carelessness causes accidents and after all they knew of the hazards and harms of the job when they took it on. So it is their problem.

Corporate executives say today that excessive death rates in mining are caused by "the men smoking too much," that false advertising claims where consumers are defrauded is not theft and therefore subject to conventional punishment, that combines and monopolies that ensure consumers pay more than they would under competition is better for them in the long run because the market is self-regulating, and that most injuries in the workplace are caused by the "dumb worker who is accident prone" (Reasons, Ross and Paterson 1981, 40-43, 139-43; Snider 1988, 251-52).

Consider the following case history. In 1987 a mineworker in Sudbury, Ontario, was charged with criminal negligence in causing the deaths of four co-workers. The worker shut off an air valve which opened a gate, sending tons of water and rock down a mine shaft, crushing and burying the men alive. The mineworker was never informed by his employer that an important by-pass air line had been inoperable for ten months. International Nickel Company (Inco) apparently knew about the faulty air valve but had not repaired it, nor had the supervisory staff advised the miners. The corporation was charged with minor violations under the Occupational Health and Safety Act of Ontario. The worker was finally acquitted in criminal court and the employer was fined $60,000. But the moral of this tale is that the powerful corporation, and its executive officers and supervisors who apparently knew about the faulty equipment faced non-criminal charges, while the unknowing miner faced criminal prosecution. (Michaud 1988, 4-6).

Studies of factory legislation, the length of the workday, and child labour laws (Carson 1980a, 1980b); clean air, water and sanitary conditions (Lambert 1973); food and drug laws (Paulus 1974); industrial pollution and poisonous waste products (Gunningham 1974); mining contracts and environmental damage (Shover 1980); environmental pollutants (Schrecker 1989); and marine disasters (Canada 1984) demonstrate that a series of deaths, injuries, moral outrages and government investigations were required before the state would act against corporate harm and wrongdoing. When it did act, criminal and administrative laws were narrow in their encroachment on corporate activity. As Szasz (1986, 15) notes, neither "individual office holders nor whole governments stay in office long if they pass legislation which, even for the best and most popular of reasons, brings to a halt industrial sectors central to the national economy." In this vein, Carson (1982) has documented how the political economy of speedy extraction of oil reserves necessary for England's position in the global economy superceded concerns for workers' health and safety and resulted in a high rate of avoidable death. In Canada, the loss of the oil-drilling rig *Ocean Ranger* and its crew was said to have resulted from priorizing immediate industrial objectives and gains over long-term marine safety. As the Royal Commission on the *Ocean Ranger* (Canada 1984, 37) notes, "the organization of command and responsibility . . . was very similar to that used in traditional land-based drilling operations [and] . . . reflected a predominant interest in an efficient industrial endeavour." The stability and safety of the rig were secondary, as was evident in the lack of qualified marine personnel, training policies and safe standard operating procedures.

The most interesting work in Canada involves the development of anticombines legislation, which was set up to prevent corporations from getting together to corner the supply of a specific market or commodity and so fix prices. Goff and Reasons (1978, 42) argue that the initiative for the original legislation in 1899 came not from the general populace but from small businessmen "who felt their firms were at the mercy of big business interests." They were annoyed at being excluded from a combine to monopolize sugar production and distribution. In addition, Smandych (1985) notes that the Act also reflected the clash of interests between labour and capital with the former seeking the elimination of combines. Given these twin threats, the state had to make a response, which took the appearance of the apparently antimonopoly, anti-big business, anticombines Act.

However, Bliss (1974), Goff and Reasons (1978), and Snider (1978) note that the anticombines legislation was totally ineffective for the first decade after enactment because the law was deliberately phrased so that the state had to prove the company had "unlawfully" as well as "unduly" and "unreasonably" violated the Act. This was legally impossible and, as Bliss (1974, 34) notes, the Act had not "the slightest effect on the wholesale Grocers Guild's price-fixing arrangements." Indeed the initial Act was the least constraining of the various drafts and, despite revisions and additions, it was a weak remedial measure, quite impotent as a regulatory instrument.

Subsequent anticombines legislation in 1910 and 1923 and many amendments after World War II sought to strengthen the law's resolve, but with little success. As a consequence of its scope, its vague wording and its weak method of enforcement, anticombines law applied to very little business conduct. As Snider (1978, 163) observes, efforts to include pro-consumer and pro-competition reforms in the legislation "were weakened or eliminated in the face of business opposition." Discussing revisions which would bolster enforcement and increase sanctions, Snider (1982, 115) also notes that:

> The financial power of those opposing the legislation was impressive — one lobbying group . . . represented 13 firms with combined revenues of 7.8 billion dollars.

The basic purpose of the anticombines law was symbolic. It was a token declaration of antimonopolism in which the interests of the powerful were enshrined in laws and regulations that had the appearance of opposing them. The government, for its part, has been a most uncertain and unreliable ally of the public interest. As Goff and Reasons (1978, 74) note, "Their public statements and their undeclared intentions were at opposite ends of the pole. . . . The two major parties in Canada (Liberal and Conservative) have attempted to render the legislation ineffective." Indeed, like antitrust legislation in the United States, anticombines legislation has been most effectively used to prosecute small businesses and labour unions (McCormick 1977; Goff and Reasons 1978; Snider 1978).

Snider's (1988) and Snider and West's (1980) analysis of commercial crime in Canada show how business interests have been able to shape regulation with regard to factory legislation; early closing by-laws; industrial relations; railways and transportation; the manufacture, sale and distribution of unsafe foods, products and drugs; the advertisement, sale or importation of unsafe articles; and weights and measures. Their analyses document the fact that, again and again, business lobbying has resulted in corporate harm, injury and suffering. Bliss (1974, 53) puts it bluntly, that "without the force of law behind them, combinations in restraint of trade remained purely voluntary agreements" to be broken at the whim of any enterprising capitalist. Of course, this is not to imply that legal gains have not been made against corporate interests. Advances have been made, and state solutions have had to accede to middle class, agrarian, and working class demands. But on matters of fundamental importance to corporations — capital accumulation and profits — they have evaded, avoided or blunted criminal law controls. As Snider (1988, 248) observes, "The laws against corporate crime were instituted in close collaboration with the corporate elite they were meant to restrain." Corporate officials find themselves, then, in a privileged position. Not only are they well poised and protected to commit their favoured types of crimes, but they are able to define which of their behaviours will be corporate crime in the first place. They have been most effective in stemming the tide of criminalization!

It is still *not* a crime under the Federal Criminal Code to conceal a workplace hazard or knowingly market an unsafe product in the United States. In 1985 a bill was introduced in the U.S. House of Representatives, providing a heavy fine and/or a prison sentence for managers who knowingly fail to inform federal agencies and affected workers or consumers about health and safety risks. The legislation was fought tooth and nail by several prominent business cartels and never made it out of the committee stage (Cullen, Maakestad and Cavender 1987, 324-25). Ralph Nader's (1970, 19-20) observation remains valid today:

Damage, perpetuated increasingly in direct violation of local, state and federal law, shatters people's health and safety but still escapes inclusion in the crime statistics. "Smogging" a city or town has taken on the proportions of a massive crime wave, yet federal and state statistical compilations of crime pay attention to "muggers" and ignore "smoggers." . . . Violations are openly flouting the laws, and an administration allegedly dedicated to law and order sits on its duties.

Taken together, these arguments suggest that powerful ideological discourses underpin the criminal law conceptions of responsibility and penality as they apply to corporate harm and wrongdoing. The law decontextualizes, depoliticizes and individualizes the accounting and sanctioning processes around corporate crime, and in turn it plays a significant role in legitimizing the different treatment accorded to corporate offenders. It is not just the attitudes and conduct of lawyers, legislators, judges and law enforcement officials that are wanting; even more fundamentally the legal system is itself ideologically predisposed to define and manage corporate harm differently and unequally (Box 1983, 9-12). Sargent (1989, 59) sums up the dilemma well:

[The] tension inheres from the premise that the moral stigma associated with prosecution and conviction for "real crimes" is intimately connected with the rhetoric of legal individualism and volunteerism expressed in the requirement of *mens rea* as an essential element of criminal responsibility. Consequently any lowering of the fault standard is assumed to result in a lessening of the social stigma associated with conviction as observed in relation to strict liability offences under regulatory statutes. Conversely, criminalizing corporate violations of regulatory statutes in order to increase the stigma associated with conviction carries the risk that convictions will become more difficult to obtain, and enforcement efforts therefore less effective. When coupled with the related view of regulatory offences as occupying a realm of conflicting values, and as being primarily concerned with illegal behavior occurring in the course of otherwise legitimate activities, rather than conduct which is itself morally approbious, it is clear that these ideological discourses play a significant role in perpetuating the preferential treatment enjoyed by corporate offenders.

But what of the corporate actors who are liable to prosecution? How are they processed through the criminal justice system? What punishments do they receive?

For the most part, corporate crimes do not fall under police jurisdiction, but under special regulatory bodies. Corporate offenses are difficult to detect. Theft, mugging or assault are forced upon a victim's attention. In contrast, the structure of most corporate activity insulates workers, consumers and the public from knowledge of their victimization. The offender and victim relationship is distant and indirect. Corporate offenders are not usually visible at the scene of the crime, and the effects of their actions are spread over time, space and populations. It is difficult to blame a corporation for lost income, environmental damage or impaired health.

In Canada, as in the United States and Britain, many agencies, inspectorates, administrations, government departments and commissions specialize in one or more types of violations in areas of consumer affairs, environment, securities, or occupational health and safety. Discussing anticombines enforcement in Canada, the Director of Investigations and Research noted that he depends largely on "complaints of violations received from consumers and businessmen and from press reports," as well as on information found by scanning financial periodicals and trade journals (Director of Investigations and Research 1975, 11). Regulatory agencies are sometimes proactive and will investigate violations on their own. As Snider (1988, 256) notes:

> For some crimes, such as false advertising, agents can discover infractions on their own merely by reading newspapers and watching television; for others, however, they must depend on public reporting, consumer groups or organizations. . . . For. . . price fixing or securities violations only insiders really know what is going on. . . . In such cases regulators must be primarily proactive [and] highly knowledgeable.

Five important points should be made about these special enforcement agencies. First, although they all have powers to initiate or recommend criminal prosecution, they are primarily regulatory bodies whose main weapon against corporate crime is administrative. They inspect premises, give warnings, negotiate, send reports, make occasional public statements, and issue orders to desist and orders of prohibition (Coleman 1989, 156; 165-69). As Kagan and Scholz (1983) point out, regulatory officials see corporate lawbreakers as "amoral calculators" who violate for profit-maximizing reasons, "politicos who have a principled opposition" to specific rules, and the "organizationally inept" who violate as a result of error or misjudgement. Only those among the first category of offenders are perceived as in need of penalty. The others are thought to require guidance. Furthermore, these agencies often are staffed by people who share many of the values of the corporate world. Herring (1936), Stanley, Mann and Doig (1967), and Graham and Kramer (1976) found that law, public service and professional administration were the primary occupations of those appointed to regulatory commissions. In the studies of the Federal Commerce Commission and the Federal Trade Commission in the United States, 64 percent of the appointments had been filled by lawyers and less than 10 percent had ties with any consumer or pro-regulation pressure groups.

Regulators identify with the industry and its problems. They generally adopt a gentle, sympathetic and educative attitude towards those they are regulating. They are hesitant, reluctant and uncertain in their enforcement effort and, by and large, they subscribe to "the bad apple in the barrel" theory that the corporate criminal is an atypical businessman (Lane 1977, 99-101; Snider 1988, 263-64). According to Fellmith (1973) the regulatory-industrial complex is also an interactive network, and one of every three regulatory officials who left their jobs were directly or indirectly employed by the industry they had been regulating. This has led many scholars to argue that the regulated industry very quickly "captures" the regulator. Cranston (1982), Hopkins (1978), Peltzman (1976) and Stigler (1975), for example, argue that regulation is quickly taken over by industry. Capital requires the powers of the state to obtain subsidies, control market entry by rivals, stabilize the market, provide economic infrastructure and valourize their policies and products. The state, through the regulatory agency, needs the resources, campaign funds, loans, technical skills and legitimacy that industry can provide. These two symbiotic needs, and not the public interest, shape the regulatory process (Snider 1988, 1990, 1991).

Second, the resources the enforcement agencies command make them a poor match for national or transnational corporations. In Britain, Canada and the United States, they are understaffed and underfunded in relation to the increasing responsibilities required of them. Box (1983, 45) reports that the factory inspectorate in the United Kingdom has a force of only 900 inspectors, who are responsible for 18 million people working in some 600,000 different locations. McMullan and Swan (1989, 294) argue that the enforcement of arson legislation in Atlantic Canada is woefully inadequate in cases involving burning for profit and insurance fraud. Understaffing, poor training and a complicated command structure make arson an easy crime to commit. Charges are laid in only 10-15 percent of cases, and convictions are obtained in less than half of these.

Caputo (1989) notes that Canada's environmental protection strategy is incoherent and uncertain. It is expressed through a bewildering body of statutes, regulations, policies and principles, and is implemented by a confusing assembly of disparate groups that lack the resources to get the job done. Schrecker (1989, 174) observes that during the twelve years the Environmental Contaminants Act was in force, the federal government of Canada, "never once used its power . . . to require toxicological testing of chemicals new to industry and commerce." Ellis (1986) reports that, compared with the United States, governments in Canada — federal, provincial and municipal — devote very few resources to collecting systematic information on corporate crime. In Ontario, the richest province in Canada, no government agency collects data on the dollar value of automobile fraud. Indeed, the federal centre for justice statistics excludes the compilation of corporate crime numbers. Snider (1982, 263) observes that if Canadian regulatory agencies were staffed at the level provided for conventional crime, "we would have one hundred times more inspectors and resources than we now have."

Moreover, in the last decade the situation has been getting worse, with staff cuts, citation drops, and legal case attritions. For example, between 1980 and 1986, the staff of the U.S. federal agencies responsible for antitrust enforcement and health and safety protection declined by 26 percent. Of the 2,533 corporate mergers reported in 1983, the Federal Trade Commission (whose record has never been impressive) investigated only thirty cases and sought but six injunctions (Coleman 1989, 165, 189). These and similar cuts and cost reductions in environmental protection, consumer safety, occupational safety and health administration and so on have resulted in near administrative paralysis, not only in the USA but in Canada and Britain (Coleman 1989, 177-80; Ellis 1986). Snider (1988, 259), for example, reports that the Restrictive Trade Commission in Canada commenced formal enquiries for only 2 percent of all complaints received, and few of these enquiries resulted in charges. Casey (1985, 108) and Sargent (1990, 106-7) conclude that a recent legal ruling by the Supreme Court of Canada in *Hunter et al.* v. *Southham News, Inc.* has effectively negated the proactive enforcement capacity of the Director of Investigation and Research under the Combines Investigations Act. In insisting on the imposition of the same conditions for the issuance of a search warrant as under the Criminal Code, and by ignoring the argument that corporate combinations require specialized techniques for detection and suppression, the powers of the director and of the criminal justice system to respond to corporate crime have been further eroded.

Third, the resources these agencies can muster to pursue corporate crime through the courts are poor and inadequate in comparison with those available to corporations. Corporations can hire the best defense — first rate lawyers, many support staff for appeals, private investigators and expert witnesses. One businessman put it this way:

> Law is like a cobweb; it's made for flies and smaller kinds of insects, so to speak, but lets the big bumblebees break through. When technicalities of the law stood in my way, I have always been able to brush them aside as easy as anything (Coleman 1989, 190).

Many former defendants have admitted that their ability to "get the best" was the decisive factor in their acquittals. Conklin (1977, 12-113) cites the example of a Texas oil magnate who gained acquittal on wiretapping charges because he spent more than $1 million on his defense. Box (1983, 46) observes that the nine corporate executives of Chemie Grunenthal who were indicted for causing bodily harm and involuntary manslaughter because of the effects of the drug thalidomide managed to have their lawyers delay and stall criminal proceedings while other lawyers worked on civil compensation. None of these executives was ever convicted.

As Braithwaite (1979b, 130) accurately notes, private and government lawyers "cannot compete with the corporation lawyers who specialize in the narrowly delimited area of 'legal loopholes'." These lawyers are experts in deflecting prosecutional attempts to obtain incriminating evidence. Their main strategy is information control, keeping evidence out of government hands by structuring access to it. By means of "adverserial information control" tactics, they invoke legal rules and precedents to deny access to company records, reports, internal memoranda, test studies, etc. and by employing "managerial information control" techniques they counsel clients holding incriminating information how to refrain from disclosing it and get the government agency to refrain from pursuing it (Cullen, Maakestad, Cavender 1987, 329). As Scott (1989, 578) notes in his study of 347 criminal corporate collusion cases, "two-thirds of those who were approached prior to the grand jury withheld documents, denied access to company records or employees, or were otherwise uncooperative." Michel Gravel, in the middle of a bribery and influence-peddling scandal, claimed that the legal tactics of his lawyers persuaded him to delay the process and eventually plead guilty. "I thought it doesn't make any difference now. I wanted to finish it, get rid of it.... There was no preliminary inquiry, there was no trial, so I never had a chance to testify at all" (*Globe and Mail*, June 22, 1991). There was also little chance of implicating others in the criminal fraud. Corporate criminals leave little to chance, and where necessary they purchase the expert testimony needed to dispute the substance of a prosecution.

Another example comes from the oil industry. In 1973 the U.S. Federal Trades Commission charged Exxon and seven other major firms with collusive actions. They sought to decentralize them into smaller and separate production, pipeline, refining and marketing companies in order to break their stranglehold on oil. The case was massive, complex and costly, consuming 12-14 percent of the FTC's budget for much of the 1970s. The oil industry's legal team delayed, stalled, obstructed and finally swamped FTC investigators with massive requests for documents and information. By 1981 the FTC finally gave up. They were hopelessly outmatched and legally outmanoeuvred. One staff attorney said the suit could be played out for "15 to 20 years after the filing of the complaint" (Coleman 1989, 184-85).

Mark Dowie (1979, 33-34) provides the following description of legal techniques used commonly, for example, in the Ford Pinto case, to counter safety standard demands:

> (a) make arguments in succession, so that the feds can be working on disproving only one at a time; (b) claim that the real problem is not x but y; (c) no matter how ridiculous each argument is, accompany it with thousands of pages of highly technical assertions that will take the government months or, preferably, years to test.

The vast power and size of the giant corporations thus lead to the paraphernalia of "The Big Case" characterized by thousands of exhibits and documents, months of hearings, and transcripts the size of telephone directories. Such cases, in the words of one veteran anticombines lawyer are "basically untryable" (Nader et al. 1976, 232). In the United States, although less so in Australia, Britain, or Canada, the problem of business resisting law enforcement has led to the formation of oppositional and criminogenic business subcultures. Vogel (1986) and Bardach and Kagan (1982), for example, write of an "organized culture of resistance," a subworld that facilitates the sharing of ideas about strategies and methods of legal resistance and counterattack. They cite example after example to show how relationships between regulators and the corporate world are running battles of citations, written directives, contestations, adversarial proceedings and low legal compliance.

Fourth, the exportation abroad of corporate crime is big business, and the regulatory agencies are increasingly unable to monitor or prosecute transnational lawbreakers who operate in shifting contexts around the globe. They have simply to move their bases of operation or their illegal rackets and activities to other states, provinces or countries where laws do not exist or are more lax (Braithwaite 1979a, 1979b, 1984; Francis 1988). As Coleman (1989, 192) observes of the United States, even the threat of moving is a particularly effective tactic against prosecutions carried on at the state or local level. "Just as Standard Oil threatened economic reprisals against the State of Missouri if it continued its anti-trust action, so numerous other businesses have threatened to leave States that pursue tough enforcement actions." Unlike regular police, regulatory officials are often instructed to put pragmatic issues such as economic loss or patriotic loyalties before the need to punish (Thomas 1982). "The inspector and even the agency," according to Snider (1987, 50), "are often in no position to assess the validity of corporate threats to declare bankruptcy or move to the Third World." These threats and actual manoeuvres put many of these corporations beyond the limits of the law, since most regulatory bodies have only geographically specific powers.

Furthermore, one country's legal system may constitute an impediment to another country's enforcement zeal. The Swiss banking system and its privacy laws provide a natural sanctuary for transnational corporations who violate legal or ethical norms through fraudulent insolvency and bankruptcy, mismanagement of funds, tax, and customs violations and false recordkeeping, and that want to keep their "dirty business" closed (Clinard 1978, 85; Francis 1988). As Clinard and Yeager (1980, 20) note:

> Because of the concentration of large-scale international banking interest, the bank secrecy laws, and its more tolerant attitude toward the type of depositors, Switzerland has undoubtedly become a center for financial transactions of a questionable nature. In such transactions deposits are laundered to obscure their illegal origins; then, through new commercial transactions, the money is made legal and is likewise concealed from tax authorities.

Similarly, the Bahamas, other Caribbean islands and Central America are secrecy havens with few corporate income taxes and extensive secrecy laws to protect transnational corporations. "You can set up bank accounts and shell corporations in a dozen jurisdictions in one day that would take police 100 years to unravel," says one RCMP white collar crime chief (quoted in Francis 1988, 61). Establishing legal controls in bribery and foreign payoff cases is extremely difficult, if not nearly impossible, as the

McDonnell-Douglas and Lockheed cases show. Both these corporations made foreign payments totalling at least $40.6 million, including substantial payments to prominent politicians in Japan, the Netherlands and Pakistan. These payments were made in order to obtain or retain business, reduce taxes, eliminate political problems, bend rules and evade the law, and induce quick official action. Bribes and payoffs are usually done through dummy or shell corporations, sales agents, and foreign subsidiaries and involve intricate concealment practices in a large number of nation-states. It is virtually impossible for regulatory bodies like the U.S. Securities and Exchange Commission (SEC) and the Internal Revenue Service (IRS) to trace them and then take unilateral action (Braithwaite 1979b, 125-42; Clinard and Yeager 1980, 168-86).

Consider the activities of the "boiler-room boys," Canadians who were operating a stock market fraud all over the world. Bankruptcy trustees discovered that many boiler rooms were linked to Panamanian dummy corporations. Tracing ownership was almost impossible. Licensing and recording rules were lax. No names were required on stock certificates, and whoever possessed them could cash them in or sell them, thus facilitating money concealment and tax evasion. Francis (1988, 62) describes the activities of one stock fraud operation as follows:

> Documents in Amsterdam showed a payment of $6.7 million from one of the boiler rooms to a Panamanian shell called Wilmington Commercial Panama. Wilmington's trust company was Citco, and its sole director was a Citco lawyer, R. Van Der Wall Arneman. Originally from Holland, Arneman is the director of 4,000 similar shell companies, which means he is the custodian of a bunch of file folders. . . . Van Apeldoorn (a Dutch bankruptcy expert) hit a brick wall trying to find out what happened to the $6.7 million payment to Wilmington Commercial Panama. In each transaction, the boiler room paid Wilmington big bucks for the stock and then resold it for considerably less. The losses were designed to bankrupt the Dutch boiler room in the end, thereby providing its owners with the opportunity to skip town, leaving behind debts to suppliers and workers and tax officials. And operating losses meant that the boiler room had no income and therefore owed no taxes in Holland. Meanwhile, the boiler room owned the Panamanian company it bought the stock from; this company made a profit but paid no taxes in Panama because there are no corporate taxes in Panama. Nice and neat. And illegal.

Fifth, the skills required to analyze evidence are different from those required to build a case against a street criminal. Corporate documents are framed in a highly specialized or technical discourse; often the research is dull, boring and academic. Pouring over company records can be a formidable assignment. Deciphering the bad from the good may not be accomplished swiftly or easily. Nor is prosecution a simple matter. Even with expertise, tenacity and familiarity with corporate documents and jargon, the task remains daunting. In addition, as Braithwaite and Geis (1982, 299) note:

> Pollution, product safety and occupational safety and health prosecutions typically turn on scientific evidence that the corporation caused certain consequences. In cases that involve scientific dispute, proof beyond a reasonable doubt is rarely, if ever, possible. Science deals in probabilities, not certainties. . . . Logically, proof beyond a reasonable doubt that a causes b is impossible. . . . The scientist can never eliminate all the possible third variables.

Beyond these constraints, prosecuting attorneys must translate highly technical testimony into a lay language for jurors to understand and for judges to comprehend and appreciate. Orland (1980, 511) notes that many judges perceive "corporate crime as victimless . . . nothing more than aggressive capitalism — a virtue, not a vice" and so are reluctant to consider unfamiliar legal rulings. Faced with ambiguity and uncertainty, they opt for narrow or strict readings of the criminal law that circumscribe events and evidence. Unsure of their legal footing, judges hesitate to view a corporation as clearly criminally culpable (Hagan and Parker 1985; Yoder 1978, 42).

This enforcement structure does little to deter corporate crime. It is seldom able to detect violations, and when it does it is most uncertain of its ability to prosecute. It has few resources to pursue the matter through the civil courts, let alone into the criminal courts, and it is outmatched and outmanoeuvred in national and international arenas. In answer to the question "Will it pay even though it is illegal?," corporate officials very often can answer "It will," since their certainty is in the likelihood of not being caught (Box 1983, 44).

But what about sanctions against corporate crime? What are the legal and social costs incurred by the corporate criminal? Studies on the enforcement of laws prohibiting certain corporate activities in America (Clinard and Yeager 1980; Coleman 1989), Canada (Casey 1985; Hagan and Parker 1985; Goff and Reasons 1978; Snider 1978, 1982; Snider and

West 1980), and Britain (Carson 1980a, 1982; Levi 1989; Cook 1989) all suggest that legal sanctions rarely deter corporate harm and theft because they are trifling rather than severe penalties and because they usually are directed at smaller, peripheral and less dangerous corporate offenders. Paulus (1974) notes that there were no convictions under the Pure Food Act from 1860 to 1872 because the Crown still had to prove *mens rea*. Carson (1980a) records that an inspectorate was not written into the early versions of British factory laws. Shover (1980) states that the strip mining law of 1977, while enforceable, was watered down to provide much less protection than the environmentalists had wanted. And Long (1979) argues that the more serious tax violators are the least likely to receive punitive sanctions for their illegalities. Even in cases where adequate laws are passed, delays in implementation or budgetary restrictions make enforcement problematic.

Goff and Reasons (1978) analyzed the enforcement of the Combines Investigation Act from 1900 to 1972 and showed very clearly how laws against corporations are not enforced and deterrence is not accomplished. Prior to 1960, no illegal mergers were successfully prosecuted, and between 1960 and 1972, of the 3,572 reported mergers, only nine cases were prosecuted and only three corporations were convicted. The penalties in two of the convictions were orders of prohibition, and in the other it was a fine of $40,000. Since 1923, only 0.003 percent of all mergers have been charged as violations of the combines laws and only 0.0005 percent of total mergers have been successfully convicted. With regard to conspiracies to combine and trade restriction violations, the government obtained eighty-four convictions, fourteen acquittals, thirty-eight "no actions" and three "no decisions" in a sixty-two-year period from 1910 to 1972. These convictions were predominantly against small and medium-sized businesses rather than against larger corporations. Snider (1978, 1988), in her studies of corporate crime in Canada, observes that between 1952 and 1975 there were eighty-nine prosecutions for conspiracy to combine or restrict trade, for resale price maintenance and predatory pricing, and for mergers and monopolies. This compares most unfavourably with 300,771 theft cases successfully prosecuted between 1949 and 1972. Of these eighty-nine prosecutions, "eight were acquitted, two were discharged at a preliminary hearing, and twenty-two of the corporations were assessed an Order of Prohibition only" (Snider 1988, 259). Not one business person was imprisoned. Only fifty-seven corporations over the 22-year period were fined, the average fine being between $7,000 and $8,000 per corporation (ibid., 259).

Similarly, studies of enforcement and sanctions in Canada for false advertising, and violations against the Food and Drugs Act, Weights and

Measures Act, Hazardous Products Act and Packaging and Labelling Act, show that, by and large, fines are small, often amount to far less than court costs and are levied against small businesses (Snider and West 1980; Snider 1982). A comparison between conventional theft offenses and the corporate crime of misleading advertising is instructive. Between 1970 and 1972, the number of cases prosecuted for theft was 56,699 (excluding Quebec and Alberta), while for misleading advertising it was 126. The numbers fined for theft was 27,217 while for misleading advertising it was 99. Finally, the numbers sentenced to prison was 11,608 for theft, and nil for those guilty of misleading advertising (Snider 1982, 251). More detailed information is provided by Ellis in his discussion of complaints of economic crimes by business corporations. He found that for the year 1982-83, the ratio of complaints to convictions was 63:1 for restraints to competition and 98:1 for marketing practices. Of the original 12,049 complaints only 190 or 1.6 percent, resulted in a conviction (Ellis 1986, 91). Focusing on Canadian securities prosecutions from 1966 to 1983, Hagan and Parker (1985) found that those offenders in positions of power committed crimes larger in scope and value than those with less power, yet they received proportionately less severe sanctions. The basic reason is because powerful corporations were less likely to be charged under the Criminal Code and more likely to be charged under the Securities Act, which carries smaller sanctions.

McCormick's (1977) analysis of antitrust enforcement in the USA from 1890 to 1969 documents the same pattern of nonenforcement and nondeterrence. Of a total of 1,551 cases, 44.7 percent were prosecuted as criminal, but only 4.9 percent of the offenders were sentenced to prison. Not one business official was imprisoned under these laws until the 1961 Heavy Electrical Conspiracy trial. Moreover, of the twenty-eight executives convicted, only seven were sent to prison, and then the maximum length of sentence was thirty days (Geis 1978, 61-64). From 1961 to 1975, only thirty-seven corporate executives out of almost 800 convicted have been imprisoned for violations of antitrust laws. The next most notorious price-fixing conspiracy was the Folding Carton case of 1976. This resulted in about one-third of those convicted being jailed, the heaviest term being fifteen days (Clinard and Yeager 1980, 278-81, 292).

An extensive study of 1,529 sanctions given to manufacturing firms in America concluded that corporations were not subjected "to the full force of the law." Almost one-half (44.2 percent) of the sanctions involved warnings only, one-fourth (24.6 percent) were "future effect orders" requiring the corporation to desist in breaking the law, and 7 percent were "retroactive orders" requiring compensatory action. Thus, fully three-quarters of the cases involved no actual penalties. Of the remainder, 21 percent were civil fines, and only 2.4 percent resulted in criminal fines. There were fifty-six cases of criminal conviction and only sixteen corporate officials served any time in jail (Coleman 1989, 166-67), and these executives were sentenced to a combined total of only 594 days of actual imprisonment. Of the total days of imprisonment, 260 days (60.6 percent) were served by two officials, who received six months each in the same case. Three others each received 30-day, 45-day and 60-day sentences. The remaining eleven averaged nine days each, and these sentences were further reduced by the judge before they had been served (Clinard and Yeager 1980, 291). The authors rightly conclude that, "the vague threat of a prison sentence will not deter executives" (ibid., 298).

The most common legal sanctions are fines and civil remedies or damages. Fines can be of two types: civil/regulatory agency fines that tend to be small and have little impact on corporate offending, and criminal fines imposed by the courts that may also be trifling but increasingly can and have been sizeable. (Shapiro 1985, 202; King 1985, 15-16; Levi 1984). For example, in the electrical conspiracy case of 1961, General Electric was fined $437,000. The maximum penalty for antitrust violations in 1980 reached $1 million. A Consumer Products Safety Commission penalty can bring a $500,000 fine. Still other agencies such as the U.S. Environmental Protection Agency (EPA) and (FTC) can impose penalties of between $10,000 to $25,000 a day for the violation of their rules and orders (Clinard and Yeager 1980, 91). Corporate fines have increased in magnitude, but calculated against hundreds of millions, and often billions, of dollars in assets and sales, even the most severe penalties are still relatively modest. According to Box (1983, 49), the heaviest corporate fine in 1961 (standardized as a fine imposed on a person earning $15,000 annually) "really was the equivalent of $12.30 and in 1976 it was $1.80!"

Furthermore, many of the corporate monetary penalties available are actually quite small. For example, fines imposed by the Occupational Safety and Health Administration are only $100, and by the Federal Drug Administration fines are $1,000 for the first offense and a total of $10,000 thereafter. Lynxwiller et al.(1983) report $993.97 as the mean fine in their study of coal mining violations, and Carson (1970) describes the fines of the British Inspectorate of Factories as miniscule. In a Canadian study, Rankin and Brown (1985, 6) found that the Waste Management Branch, using criminal law, convicted an annual average of sixteen offenders with an average fine of $565 while interestingly the Workman's Compensation Board was more successful using administrative penalties, fining offenders an average of $3,100. Schrecker (1984), in his study of the political economy of environmental hazards in Canada, was forced to conclude that "sanctions are applied lightly and infrequently" against environmental and workplace crime.

Although, in theory, fines represent a type of penalty, corporate fines rarely even equal the amount of profit made from illegal behaviours. Four-fifths of the fines in the Clinard study, mentioned above, were for less than $5,000. Moreover, the size of the fines did not increase with the size of the offender. The median fine against the smaller firms was $750, for the medium-sized firms it was $1,650, and for the larger firms it was only $1,000. Snider's (1987, 257-59) research in Canada showed that in 1975 the average fines for food and drug Act violations were $225 per charge and $291 per case, for hazardous products Act violations they were $50 per charge and $50 per case, and for weights and measures Act violations $273 per charge and $625 per case. For misleading advertising in the years from 1970 to 1974, the average fine was $812 per case, for price misrepresentation in the years from 1962 to 1974 the most common fine per case was $100, and for industrial harm and death in 1973-74, the average fine per charge was $977. Between 1980 and 1983, the median fine levied against corporate criminals in Canada was $1,200 (Ellis 1986, 92). With few exceptions, the fines are modest and may be compared to "additional license fees" for engaging in illegal conduct. As Coleman (1989, 167) rightly observes, "a $1,000 fine against a multibillion dollar corporation cannot be said to constitute a punishment in any realistic sense of the word." Even the most severe legal sanctions must be thought of in the context of corporate costs and benefits. As Gross (1978b) notes:

> The $7 million fine which was levied against the Ford Motor Company for environmental violations was certainly more than a slap on the wrist, but it rather pales beside the estimated $250 million loss which the company sustained on the Edsel. Both represent environmental contingencies which managers are paid high salaries to handle. We know they handled the latter.... One can only infer that they worked out ways to handle the fine too.

Fines as currently levied seem to be best understood as the added cost of doing business.

Nor do civil damages seem particularly effective in controlling corporate deviation and criminality. Like fines, their absolute size may be large, but when measured against their gross revenues they are often relatively insignificant. Furthermore, from the victim's point of view, they are frequently outgunned by highly paid corporate lawyers and subjected to lengthy and costly legal battles. Corporations such as Ford, Firestone, Richardson-Merrill and others have been quite effective in legally outmanoeuvring or limiting civil suits. For example, the Johns Manville Corporation, the largest manufacturer of asbestos, declared bankruptcy in 1982. Despite strong profits and billions of dollars in assets, the company claimed it could not pay all the potential civil judgements against it. Similarly, A.H. Robins has "legally stonewalled" the victims of the Dalkon Shield. It declared bankruptcy in 1985 and the more than 5,000 lawsuits pending against the company have been frozen (Sherrill 1987, 56). The value of civil remedies as a deterrent is primarily symbolic and uncertain. As Coleman (1989,1760) notes:

> civil action still takes many years, and many victims are forced to agree to quick settlements. . . . Moreover, victims . . . cannot for one reason or another prove their case. Thus, it is quite common for a few victims to receive huge settlements and for many others to get nothing.

The studies mentioned above and many others (Carson 1970; Clinard and Yeager 1980; Hopkins 1980; Thomas 1982; Schrecker 1984; Levi 1989; Cook 1989) all support the view that little deterrence is created by the typical sanctions imposed on corporations and their offending officials. Cook's (1989, 126) observation about tax fraud deterrence has wide application. "Wealth and enterprise exculpate the rich," while "poverty itself inculpates the poor." There is some sparse evidence, however, that criminal convictions and fines may operate as a specific deterrent, but usually to deter corporations from recommitting the same offense (Box 1983,52; Clinard and Yeager 1980,294). By and large, there are few sharp judicial teeth to arouse a fear of detection or penalty in corporate executives. The judiciary treats the matter leniently, often concluding that the acts of prosecution and conviction are punishment enough (Clinard and Yeager 1980, 89-292; Hagan and Parker 1985). The corporation, by and large, forgives the crime. For example, the board of directors of Gulf Oil took two and one-half years to dismiss the chairperson of the board and the chief executive officer after it learned of their illegal payments of $100,000 to the Nixon re-election campaign and $4 million to the political party supporting Korean President Park. During those two and one-half years, "there was no evidence that the directors had pressed hard to learn who in management had been responsible for authorizing the illegal payments" (Clinard and Yeager 1980, 308). The individual is almost always dispensable, and should a "responsible" individual be imprisoned "then another organizational man will replace him . . . while others try to clean up the problem he has created" (ibid., 298). Some companies have a special post for a person to take the blame:

the "vice-president responsible for going to jail." Braithwaite (1984, 308) puts it as follows:

> Lines of accountability had been drawn in the organization such that if there were a problem and someone's head had to go on the chopping block, it would be that of the "vice-president responsible for going to jail."

Thus there are few public claws to threaten corporate executives in their lawbreaking activities. Nothing much happens to them by way of public scandal and social ruin. Though some are fired and others may have their salaries temporarily reduced, most retain their jobs, have others cover for them, and hold onto lucrative retirement benefits. Fines and damages often are paid for by the corporation by others. For example, in the case of the continuing illegal contract-bidding scandal in Ottawa concerning illegal kickbacks and fraud, Michel Gravel's $50,000 fine was paid anonymously. Gravel did not put up the money for his fine, but he believes that the Conservative Party looked after him and paid his legal costs (*Globe and Mail*, June 22, 1991). For some, the crime may even be a step towards career advancement. In many instances, corporations are so reluctant to dismiss guilty officials that they soon re-employ them, sometimes with higher salaries and better benefits than previously. Consider the following cases (Clinard and Yeager 1980, 295-96; Geis 1978; Vandivier 1978):

- Two prominent executives involved in consumer fraud in the Goodrich disc-brake scandal were later given promotions and salary increases despite being charged and convicted.
- An oil corporation executive who had been fined and fired because of a bribery conviction was retained as a consultant at an annual salary of $150,000.
- Of twenty-one corporate executives who were fined or imprisoned for making illegal campaign contributions, twelve hold their preconviction corporate positions, five resigned or retired, two served as consultants and two were dismissed. Three corporate chairmen retained their positions at $335,000, $314,000 and $212,000 a year, respectively.
- The board of directors of Fruehauf Corporation did not dismiss the chairman or president of the corporation after they were convicted of conspiracy to evade $12.3 million in federal excise taxes. They were retained as consultants and paid $440,000 and $200,000 in salaries and bonuses.

- In the electrical conspiracy case of the 1960s one convicted offender wasfired from his $125,000-a-year position, only to be hired on release from prison by another corporation. Others were rehired at higher salaries than when they were convicted.

This practice of corporate musical chairs has few adverse occupational consequences for corporate officials. It also signals to the offenders that being guilty before the courts carries little social censure. Consider the case of Revco Drug Stores Inc., one of the largest discount drug chains in the world. In 1977, Revco was convicted of fraudulently obtaining over one-half million dollars in medicaid payments from a state public welfare department agency funded by taxpayers. Because of computer problems at Revco, 50,000 claims were rejected at the welfare department and went unpaid. The company determined that the cost of correcting and re-submitting the rejected claims was more than the worth of the claims, so they innovated unlawful solutions. Two executives hired a clerical staff of six and instructed them to fabricate claims according to the acceptable standards of the welfare department. Revco received its reimbursements, but the fraud was discovered and the company was fined $50,000 and ordered to pay restitution in the amount of $500,000. The two executives were fined $2,000 each. Four years later Revco applied for and received an expungement order that allowed its criminal record to be destroyed (Vaughan 1983, 1-19).

Media indignation about corporate crime is slowly growing, as is public concern, but mild sentences foster the idea that such crimes are "technical mistakes." Few corporate consciences are outraged and scandalized. Though public concern and sentiment has grown about the harm and cost of corporate criminality, executive offenders do not seem to experience much social disrepute. Geis (1978, 283) reports that convicted corporate conspirators were elected to prominent honorary positions in industry and the community. They continued to be regarded as "upright and steadfast... [and] as solid and substantial citizens." Sherrill (1987, 56) notes that E. Claiborne Robins, Sr., the President of A.H. Robins, was hailed as a civic leader by the president of the University of Virginia. "Your example will cast its shadow into eternity, as the sands of time carry away the indelible footprint of your good works. We applaud you for always exhibiting a steadfast and devoted concern for your fellow man. Truly, the Lord has chosen you as one of His most essential instruments." Fisse and Braithwaite (1983), in their international survey of corporate crime, concluded that involvement in corporate crime resulted in little more than temporary embarrassment. McBarnet (1991), in her study of tax fraud, discovered that tax violators played with, or worked on, the boundaries of the law, manipulating it to their advantage so the "labelled" were in fact in control of the censuring process. The craft of law and the post hoc use and contrivance of tax legislation allowed "high net worth" corporate tax violators to escape the risk of social control and criminal stigma. Simon and Eitzen (1986, 59-60) observed that the news media, themselves made up of corporations, have ignored or trivialized corporate crime, thus promoting little popular disapproval and public shame. Snider (1982) discovered that corporate theft does much more damage to the social order in Canada than does conventional theft, but the written legal sanctions and the enforcement practices result in much less social censure. Cynicism mounts and moral anger declines. As Geis (1978, 283) notes, "Wearied by expected exposé, citizens find their well of moral indignation has long since run dry." This lack of community indignation benefits the corporate criminal.

   In these circumstances, executives feel free to commit corporate crimes. Not surprisingly, they do not, for the most part, think of themselves as criminals, nor do they usually feel morally responsible or legally liable for the harm they cause. When it comes to feeling little remorse, A.H. Robins is exemplary. In a courtroom confrontation between Federal Judge Miles Lord and three senior A.H. Robins officials, the president of the company responded to the long legal reprimand of their actions with strong silence. Justice Lord charged that A. H. Robins, "without warning to women invaded their bodies by the millions and caused them injuries by the thousands." He further argued that when the time came for these women to make claims against A.H. Robins, they were attacked.

> You inquired into their sexual practices and into the identity of their sex partners. You exposed these women — and ruined families and reputations and careers — in order to intimidate those who would raise their voices against you. You introduced issues that had no relationship whatsoever to the fact that you planted in the bodies of these women instruments of death, of mutilation, of disease. . . . you've got lives out there, people, women, wives, moms and some who will never be moms.... you are the corporate conscience. Please, in the name of humanity, lift your eyes above the bottom line(quoted in Perry and Dawson, 1985).

   A few weeks later, E. Claiborne Robins, Jr., described Judge Lord's speech as a "poisonous attack" and left the intrauterine device on the market. Giving deposition in 1984, one of the senior vice-presidents was asked if any officer or company employee had admitted sorrow or remorse about infections and damages caused by the Dalkon Shield. He answered, "I've never heard anyone make such remarks because I've never heard anyone that said the Dalkon Shield was the cause" (quoted in Perry and Dawson 1985). Other executives, calculating the social risks of undertaking illegal but profitable actions, will likely conclude that their jobs, family, friends and reputations will not be put much at risk. In one interview, for example, Michel Gravel confirmed that his construction firm was doing well despite his conviction on fifteen counts of fraud and influence peddling. "During all those years we never lost credibility with our bankers and the people we did business with" (*Globe and Mail*, June 22, 1991). The editor of one newspaper writes wryly:

> If you're going to steal money . . . take big amounts and do it with a pen or a computer, not a gun. That's the safest way to do it; you don't have to worry about getting shot by a policeman and you don't have to worry about going to prison if you get caught. . . . E.F. Hutton pleaded guilty [2,000 counts] to criminal fraud charges involving an elaborate scheme to overdraw bank chequing accounts and deprive banks of millions in interest. The company was ordered to pay a $2 million fine, but no one went to jail. . . . The impression is with the public that if you rob a service station of $25, you're going to prison. But if you're with a big brokerage firm and you rob millions of dollars, nothing is going to happen to you (quoted in Cullen, Maakestad and Cavender 1987, 341).

The interplay between capital accumulation and the organizational structure of corporate bureaucracy is central to understanding corporate crime (see Figure 1). The contradictions between corporation goals and the needs of competitors, employees, consumers, the public and the state set up powerful uncertainties in the working environment of corporations. The motives to commit corporate crime are thus rational solutions to this dilemma. Motives are transformed into corporate criminal behaviour by the ideology, gender polarity and subculture of corporate bureaucracy and by the nature of legal sanction. But why is the law so inept at controlling crimes of the powerful? Why is there so little law and order in the corporate suites and boardrooms? In order to answer these questions we need to examine, briefly, the role of the state.

The state is not a neutral and independent entity. It is not above society, arbitrating social conflicts. Its history and development is such that it is closely allied with the process of capital accumulation. The role of the state is broadly determined by the existing structure of society.

Thus there are close encounters and connections between the state and the corporate sector of the dominant class (Clement 1975, 1977). By promoting capital growth, the state is not only assisting business interests and activities, it is also performing its essential function of guaranteeing the long term reproduction of the economic system as a whole (Pearce 1978, 61). According to Heilbroner (1985, 104) the key inputs from the state to the regime of capital include: (1) economic liberalization in the encouragement of free movement of goods, service and labour within national territories, (2) economic orchestration such as planning and social crises intervention, (3) provision of economic infrastructure such as transportation networks and a trained labour supply, (4) intervention for social consensus (backed by force) in ameliorating the disruptive effects of the capital accumulation process and (5) the management of external relations including trade, financial arrangements, property rights, and war. As Heilbroner (1985, 104) observes, "The market system would be unsustainable without [these] socializing, protecting, and stimulating state activities."

Figure 1. The Context of Corporate Crime

Furthermore, the microeconomy of the state — its own fiscal base — is in large measure, dependent upon the continuous flow of capital accumulation, part of which it usurps in the form of corporate taxes and part of which it borrows from private sector capital. Thus, laws against corporate activities are regarded with the greatest of circumspection because of the economic liabilities these laws may create. As we have seen, most laws regulating corporate activities in Canada were passed with the tacit cooperation of the corporate elite. They came about primarily "because state intervention [was] the only means of ending a competitive situation from which none of the competitors were benefitting" (Bliss 1974, 39, 40-42, 130). This might be termed legal regulation for capital. Laws defining property rights and the exchange of property would be central regulatory areas. Thus, land and patent laws, laws governing access to natural resources and defining rights of investors and financiers, tax laws, anticombines and restraint of trade laws, and regulatory laws determining fair practice versus theft or fraud all tend to institutionalize, enhance or protect the basic economic relations of production and the distribution of wealth in society.

The relationship between the state and the corporate world is dialectical. The real and perceived interests of capital shape everyday government disclosure at every level, and in turn the state tries to ensure the profitability of private capital by providing economic development grants, income tax benefits, corporate infrastructure, subsidized transportation, 'free' loans and other corporate incentives (Offe 1982; Gough 1979).

The state also intervenes in what may be called the legal regulation of labour and labour power. These laws define the rights and obligations of producers and labourers involved in specific economic activities. Thus contract law, industrial relations law, and health and safety legislation set limits and define "freedoms" for the use of labour power. Finally, the state uses laws of public order — usually criminal in nature — to control the conduct of individuals outside the spheres of production and the reach of social institutions. These laws are primarily aimed at (1) disciplining behaviours that are disruptive and potentially dangerous to social peace such as assault and interpersonal violence, rape, vagrancy, making a public nuisance and drug use and (2) controlling behaviours that violate specific public norms such as those related to vice, censorship, liquor use, and morals. Thus the role of the state is multidimensional, complex and contradictory. It is itself a contested terrain where diverse interests compete, but it must be recognized that the "unequal structure of representation" within the state favours the interests of large transnational capital. Heilbroner (1985, 105) described this relation between the corporate sector and the state as one "in which capital calls the tune by which the state normally dances but takes for granted that the state will provide the theatre within which the performance takes place."

Besides performing its basic functions of facilitating capital accumulation and maintaining social peace, the state seeks to secure a belief in its own legitimacy. "The hand of the state . . . is also stayed by notions of fairness, and justice, as well as political expediency" (ibid., 84). The state is thus more than simply a pliant tool of corporate capital. It possesses and exercises relative autonomy, and it may under certain circumstances act against or appear to act against individual corporate interests. The state's claim to credibility is buttressed by its willingness and ability to pursue a separate objective that entails not only catering to and protecting the regime of capital but also regulating corporate conduct. This makes the state a "site of conflict and struggle" in which laws promoting public, worker, environmental, humanitarian and consumer interests (e.g., laws to control corporate harm and wrongdoing) may stand in contradiction to those promoting private interests (e.g., corporate concentration and monopolies, corporate taxation and product liability) (Ratner, McMullan, Burtch 1987). By calculations of prudence, the state must decide how and when it will intervene in corporate matters. Devoting too many resources to capital accumulation may jeopardize its claims to public representativeness and thus undermine its societal legitimacy. However, the regulation of corporate power may strengthen the hand of the state because notions of economic justice and fairness will be trumpeted. Thus, for example, in the presence of strong and organized social movements, the interests of sectors of capital may have to be compromised to trade union demands for safety equipment, health protections and improved working conditions or to environmental demands for pollution-free communities. When contradictions become visible, and where beliefs about social justice are promoted, legitimation issues may be legally managed by specifying minimum fetters on the operation of capital. The corporate elite, however, may be displeased and fight back.

To return to the question of corporate crime: Has the state, through law, acted primarily with reference to the interests of capital? The answer, I believe, is a qualified yes. Studies by Pearce (1978), McCormick (1979) and Barnett (1981) in the United States, Young (1974), Goff and Reasons (1978), Snider (1978, 1982), Casey (1985) and Smandych (1985) in Canada, and Hopkins (1979) in Australia came to remarkably similar conclusions that may be summarized as follows:

- The origin of laws against corporate monopolies and mergers was by and large the product of intra-capitalist conflict, manifested in the struggle between small business interests and growing corporate capital. Rarely did big business introduce these types of laws.

- In cases where legislation emerged because of the demands of labour against unjust accumulation of aggregated wealth, the state has acted to resolve the conflict by "neutralizing" or "displacing" the conflict through the passing of symbolic laws. This did little to control corporate crime, but it did have the effect of legitimizing the state by convincing the public at large that something was being done about price-fixing, mergers and misleading advertising.

- Much anticorporation lawmaking did little to restrain the continuing control of the corporate elite over the political and economic sectors of society. This was an intended consequence. The effect was to "protect" rather than to interfere with the interests of capital. As Pearce (1978, 87) notes, business corporations actually cooperated with the state in shaping anticombines laws because it afforded "a means by which monopoly capital could be achieved against dangerous competitors."

- The laws against corporate harm, danger and theft deliberately were made vague, ineffectual and unenforceable (Young 1974, 73, Goff and Reasons 1978; Snider 1987). Well-written legislation and effective enforcement might deter crime but it would also inhibit capital accumulation. As Barnett (1981, 7) observed, the enactment and enforcement of product safety laws, environmental, anticombines, and union labour laws could not be made "so severe as to diminish substantially the contribution of large corporations to growth and employment." Efforts to reform and strengthen enforcement and sanctions were continually resisted by corporate opposition. The state acquiesced, repeatedly watering down its own proposals.

- Civil and/or administrative laws that cover most corporate injury, killing and theft and criminal laws that cover the same behaviours when they are committed by citizens generally differ because they serve two very different functions. According to Glassbeek (1989, 128) and Snider (1979; 1982, 253), the state passes criminal laws to repress and deter. The underlying logic is to reduce the strains inherent in the inequality of the economic system. The emphasis is on controlling the attitudes, behaviours, demeanour and background of untoward offenders or of the underclass. These persons are most likely to become entangled with the criminal law and its regime of punishment. The laws of corporate crime have a very different raison d'etre. The criminal law seldom is applied to business corporations because the corporate elite who constitute a dominant force within the ruling class of society never intended it to be used against their actions, however injurious and costly they might be (Glassbeek 1989). The underlying logic of laws against corporate crime is largely one of image-making. The intent is not instrumental but rather regulating through "statutes designed to make it appear that the state is acting . . . to retain the integrity of the liberal democratic system" (Snider 1982, 253). Because of intimate ties and dependencies between corporations and the state, the latter has little "vested interest in controlling those they are forced to regulate" (ibid., 253). The state is reluctant to fashion legal sanctions with sharp judicial teeth. Nor have they been pushed very hard to extend or enforce corporate crime laws. The absence of law and order campaigns against corporate violations and harm has allowed many states to be complacent.

- In the few instances where corporate capital was not successful in shaping the content of legislation because the balance of class forces resulted in counter-lobbying by consumers, small business or labour, the state believed that ultimately they were ensuring long-term systematic interests, even though they were acting against the short-term interests of specific business groups (Hopkins 1979, 79-80).

From the available evidence, it seems fair to conclude that the law is inept because it has been well conceived to be so. Statutes are weak and lax, enforcement budgets are small, sanctions are miniscule and regulatory regimes are ineffective precisely because corporate capital has had a strong hand in shaping state policy. On matters as important as the conditions for capital accumulation, the exploitation of labour power and the maximization of profits, it is difficult to imagine that national states and their control agencies will be able to free themselves from their obligations to the interests of corporate capital. Though they have made some reforms and increased penalties for corporate crime, it is the corporate small fry that have been penalized, while the bigger fish have been allowed to grow into omnivorous sharks. The irony, of course, is that the worst offenders are transnationals. In the United States, the largest firms are the most criminal and those that dominate the oil, pharmaceutical, and motor vehicle industries are "the most likely to violate the law" (Clinard and Yeager 1980, 119). Similarly, Snider (1978) and Goff and Reasons (1978) found that companies who did *not* dominate markets or who were small to medium-sized were much more likely to receive enforcement orders. But those corporations who set prices and had major economic power were "free to engage in their monopolistic practices" and fix prices (Goff and Reasons 1978, 86). The big ones get away, because they seldom are in the net!

When it is realized that car manufacturers, oil conglomerates, petrochemical industries and pharmaceutical companies are among the largest corporations in the world, it can be appreciated that the interests of corporate capital are international and their leverage on national states is worldwide (Braithwaite 1984; Clinard and Yeager 1980). Not surprisingly, these giant corporations export corporate crime all over the globe, and especially to Third World countries. They opt for legal evasion in countries where labour costs, safety, environmental concerns, and product quality controls are either absent or less stringent, and where emergent or already peripheralized nation-states are more dependent upon capital and have even fewer resources to circumvent corporate illegalities (Braithwaite 1979a, 1979b, 1984; Michalowski and Kramer 1987).

Nation-states have seldom possessed the ability to control corporate criminality. Though specific and limited objectives have been achieved, most nation-states have danced to the tune that capital has called. The problem is that the theatres that governments have conveniently provided now know no national boundaries. The repertoires, scenes and settings are today international. This, as we shall see, poses some difficult problems in determining strong and effective, and, necessarily, radical remedies.

• 5 •
Proposals for Capitalist Punishment

I have argued that corporate crime is a serious and enduring form of criminality. The scope, harm, and social and economic costs are enormous and driven by the "logics" of capital accumulation and bureaucratic immorality. The law and the state are implicated in the reproduction of corporate crime and rarely in its abolition. The reader may be excused for feeling pessimistic about how corporate crime can be combatted. The remedies are not obvious or certain and the playing field upon which change must occur is not level. Control of the crimes of the powerful must be well considered and strategic. Movement needs to be made on many fronts simultaneously. What is to be done about law and order and corporate crime?

One blunt answer is: "Nothing! No change is possible or will make one bit of difference. Only when the means of production and distribution are transformed and fully socialized will the incidence and scope of corporate crime diminish." But, short of a nuclear disaster, capitalism is not likely to disappear in our lifetimes. Nor may we be satisfied with the radical hope for an inevitable rosy future. Conjuring or invoking the millenium, however promising and progressive, will not do. But must we stand on the sidelines just because the dice are "loaded" or the game is "fixed"? Is it justifiable to turn away or throw up our arms in the face of such corporate pillage and carnage? Perhaps strategic reforms can be won and, in turn, they may be prefigurative to an alternative and effective control policy. Something good might be achieved from corporate regulation, at least in principle. As Box (1983, 65) notes, "If hundreds of corporation-caused deaths can be prevented, if thousands of occupational diseases and injuries can be avoided, and if millions of pounds stolen by corporations can be saved, then it would be no bad achievement."

Several hopeful signs are on the horizon despite the gloom of the situation. The first is an optimism of will. In the United States and Canada, awareness and condemnation of corporate crime is growing. Since the late 1970s attitudes have changed. Growing is the assurance that justice can prevail, that apathy can be turned into enthusiasm, and dishonesty into decency. According to Cullen and Dubeck (1985), Cullen, Link and Polanzi (1982), Cullen, Mathers, Clark and Cullen (1983) and Sinden (1980) the seriousness rating of business crime "particularly violence (resulting in death or injury) and price fixing," has increased "both absolutely and to a greater extent" than any other crime category. Public indignation is mounting. Popular attitudes are hardening and becoming less tolerant towards crimes in the suites. As Anderson (1981, 28) has noted, a growing demand is that "corporate fatcats, whose profit-motivated decisions cause death or injury to thousands be punished at least as severely as a ghetto kid who holds up a neighborhood liquor store." A study by Schrager and Short (1980, 26) concluded that "corporate crimes with physical impact" were viewed by the public as more serious than ordinary street crime, and that the public is as concerned about controlling corporate crime as it is about stopping street crime. In Canada, a study by Goff and Mason-Clark (1989, 31) confirms the increase in the seriousness rating of corporate harm and injury, especially where violence is thought to have occurred.

Hills (1987), Katz (1980) and Cullen, Maakestad and Cavender (1987) suggest that a social movement against corporate crime has emerged. These authors argue that attitude changes reflect the publicity surrounding the Ford Pinto scandal, the pricing practices of oil companies, various corporate homicide trials, notorious price-fixing and price-gouging schemes, and a multitude of occupationally related health and safety transgressions. Corporate crime, we are told, is now under attack from unionists, environmentalists, native organizations, consumer groups, public interest law lobbies, feminists, socialists and others involved in rights struggles. Over time, these groups have delegitimated the corporate structure, to some degree, creating a confidence gap in major economic institutions. In the process, latent community hostilities towards corporate harm and wrongdoing have been unleashed. A brimstone smell now surrounds corporate offenses in a way not possible twenty years ago, with lawyers and academic criminologists contributing to the "revitalization movement" against corporate crime (Geis 1973; Kramer 1989). As Hagan (1987, 334) notes of Canada, "there is some evidence that the mid 1970's brought a new and somewhat harsher attitude toward the issue of white collar crime. . . . This new concern seems at least in part to have been a response to incidents such as . . . Watergate and the Canadian experience with Harbourgate." Harbourgate received national media attention, involved some of Canada's largest corporations and tainted the highest levels of government with misconduct and corruption charges. In 1979, five corporate executives were found guilty and jailed for two to five years and the corporations were fined a total of $6.5 million (Larsen 1981, 23-29). The Gravel Affair of 1988-89 and the revelations about illegal kickback schemes and bid-rigging on state contracts has intensified public disgust with corporate wrongdoing and political crime. An ideological space has been opened for meaningful reform. Victim consciousness has been raised to the point that a practical, moral critique now challenges the corporate state, the corporation and the uncaring instrumental reasoning that guides its policy and politics. As Snider (1987, 57) observes:

> Successful ideological struggles have "upped the ante" for the corporate sector; that is, they have increased the price of legitimacy for the corporation, by raising the standards of corporate behaviour necessary to secure public acceptance. This has resulted in new definitions of "reasonable" business behaviour, new standards of corporate morality against which transgressions are assessed, and a series of new limits on tactics which are acceptable to maximize profits and risks which are legitimate for employees.

The effects of the attack on corporate crime have been minimal. Nevertheless, a countervailing social movement is in place, willing and able to fight for social and legal changes in this realm which "affects the longevity, health and ease of life for millions on a daily basis" (ibid., 57). This was not true in 1960. But in the 1990s, "law and order in the suites" is a social program with political purchase and promise.

The raising of public awareness and victim consciousness has been achieved by its incorporation as a function of controlling and regulating agencies. The increased number of media investigations and documentaries about corporate crime have produced a greater sensitivity to its harms and have become a catalyst for stronger and broader innovative social control programs (Kramer 1989, 153-55). Certainly the collective ignorance, misinformation, cynicism and mystification about corporate crime reported in public opinion polls of the 1960s and 1970s, no longer holds (Box 1983, 15-19). Survey after survey demonstrate that corporate crimes such as price-fixing and violations of trust as well as those involving physical harm are perceived by the public as morally offensive and deserving of the "use of the criminal sanction for such misconduct" (Schlegel 1988, 628). Opinion polls now reveal that popular thinking and sentiment are in favour of much tougher laws, regulations and sanctions on corporate misconduct than the state seems able or willing to deliver (Coleman 1989). Further, state policies that would roll back standards for environmental protection, workplace safety and consumer protection are consistently opposed (Cahan and Moskowitz 1985, 25).

A second glimmer of light in the dark discourse surrounding corporate crime control is that the state and its criminal justice system, including civil and administrative bodies, are increasingly receptive to the deterrance of corporate crime. A recent ruling by an Alberta court in Canada has placed the cost of environmental obligations above the rights of creditors in a precedent-setting bankruptcy case. The Alberta Court of Appeal held that a bankrupt oil Company must spend money to clean up potentially hazardous well sites before a creditor receives money from the closure of the corporation. Environmental liability would seem to take precedence over a secured creditor. Lending institutions such as banks and trust companies may now have to consider environmental risks as well as financial prospects before they loan capital (*Globe and Mail*, July 12, 1991).

The law has also "edged increasingly toward holding corporations criminally culpable for socially harmful conduct." (Cullen, Maakestad and Cavender 1987, 310-11). New reckless homicide statistics, legal case precedents and changes in legal attitudes have bolstered criminal prosecutions and criminal sentencing. Glassbeek (1989) claims that Canadian Criminal Code statutes on criminal negligence and manslaughter ought to be used against corporate employers where workers are injured or killed as a result of reckless or negligent corporate decisions in the workplace. He compares violations of mandatory safety standards with dangerous or impaired driving and concludes that convictions in the corporate world should be based on a similar principle (where the necessary *mens rea* is established) by a finding of reckless disregard of risk to human life and limb. Pearce and Tombs (1990, 430-33) extend this comparison between corporate law and motoring law and conclude that the duties-of-care regulations should be made similar. "Reckless employing" should be given the same weight as "reckless driving." Strict liability should not be displaced by common-sense notions of culpability. Ignorance is no defense and, if a corporation cannot do business without causing injury to employees, its executives should be fined or imprisoned and the corporation risk eventual disqualification. Criminal liability, negligence and sanctions must be strengthened if harm-causing conduct closely allied to private profit-making are to be curbed. The Ford Pinto trial, according to Cullen, Maakestad and Cavender (1987, 311), "would not have taken place a decade or two earlier." And Schlegel (1988) notes that deterrence and deserts are justifiable and compatible goals of corporate punishment. The dismissal of retribution as an aim of corporate criminal sanctions, he argues, is short-sighted. When retribution is viewed more broadly to include reprobation and censure, then the use of punishment against corporate wrongdoing is grounded in notions of justice and fairness. Accordingly, "there is nothing unique about corporate crime that would exclude retribution . . . as a justification for punishment." (ibid., 631)

The state criminal justice system, as we have seen, seeks to project itself above social conflicts and expects to be recognized as fair and just because it is guided by universal principles that transcend sectoral interests. The state, despite its bias, is not a monolithic structure. It is an arena of conflict and struggle, and contradictions between principles and judicial practices may be exploited advantageously for victims of corporate crime. A forceful demonstration that the law and the administration of justice is failing to live up to its professed principles may have a positive result of shaming its principals into action. Many recent criminal prosecutions in America and Canada have had the effect of pushing the state and its legal institutions to act consistently with their own principles, and in doing so they have highlighted the contradictions between stated goals and actual practices. Claims to equality before the law and to protection, safety and security are difficult to maintain if the state treats corporate offenders leniently and does little to protect its citizens from predatory corporations.

> Revelations of overseas payoffs, illegal campaign contributions, charges of recklessly endangering workers, and the wanton dumping of toxic chemicals — to name only a few examples — created a dark picture of business executives. In this context, it was not unusual to think that corporations were criminals who should be sanctioned stringently (Cullen, Maakestad and Cavender 1987, 33).

Publicizing these and other corporate crimes has caused a legitimacy gap of increasing proportions and, according to Snider (1987; 1991), Hills (1987), Katz (1980) and Rakoff (1985), the criminal justice system is moving, if only slightly, to close the confidence gap between principles and practices. Cullen, Maakestad, and Cavender (1987, 335-36) put it best:

.....society has shifted its moral boundaries between what is considered to be acceptable or unacceptable corporate conduct. ...The [new] moral or ideological context which made corporate prosecutions seem feasible, if not obligatory, will not be eroded substantially in the near future ... [also] the prospects are bright for future attempts to criminally sanction corporate misconduct. ... Further. .. prosecutions themselves will help to sustain the very context which made them possible. .... The result, which now seems to be in process, is that efforts at social control escalate; corporate trials strengthen emergent moral boundaries, which in turn create new pressures for holding corporations criminally liable.

A final note of optimism comes from recent efforts to develop new strategies for controlling corporate crime. There is "much ado about something" in these proposed solutions: shaming and positive repentence, new legal tools and controls, corporate accountability and restructuring, new forms of penalty and criminal sanctioning, and the application of countervailing force against corporate crime. Because employees, consumers and other victims of corporate crime are having their consciousness sharpened and raised by new social movements around labour, women, consumerism and environmentalism, and because the state and its legal institutions are being shamed into closing the gap of unequal representation to ensure their own credibility and legitimacy, maybe some modest proposals for "capitalist punishment" could be put into effective operation. Cullen, Maakestad, and Cavender (1987, 345) are cautiously optimistic:

> Times have changed enough that criminal penalties are being viewed as contingencies, which organizations must begin to address. ... The Pinto case is suggestive here. Nine months after being indicted on charges of reckless homicide, Ford took steps to introduce organizational reform. This reform emphasized product "durability, quality, and reliability" and instructed management to "look beforehand at points of no return," such as when designs for fuel systems are finalized and when machines are tooled. The problems besetting the production of the Pinto were to be avoided in the future.

Consensus seems to be growing that corporate criminals can be deterred, because their crimes are essentially rational and instrumental. Their illegalities are seldom acts of passion or situational opportunism but flow instead from calculated cost/benefit risk taking. Corporate criminals have little emotional commitment to their crimes. Nor are corporate executives nearly as committed to crime as a way of life as many serious conventional criminals are, so desisting from criminal involvement does not entail loss of social role and a change in lifestyle for them. But corporate executives do have a high stake in conformity and respectability. The potential costs of legal violation may be high: loss of social status, respectability, a well-paying job, property and life's comfortable amenities (Box, 1983, 67; Fattah 1976; Geis 1973,193-96). Similarly, corporations are very much in the business of manufacturing and presenting a favourable image of themselves and their products so they might flourish and capital might grow. They worship at the altar of the positive image. The idea that the *Fortune* 500 list might be replaced with a *Fortune* Most Wanted List would be an unwelcome message. Consequently, on the surface at least, both corporations and their officials "would be more deterrable than actual or potential criminals from other levels of society" (Cullen, Maakestad and Cavender 1987, 344). But how?

The history of penal practice is a graveyard of used and not-so-used sanctions. Shaming, repentance and atonement are some practices. There was a period of time when the wayward were publicly humiliated and decried, when self-confessions accompanied with displays of repentance and atonement were deemed necessary steps on the path towards social reintegration. Those measures, of course, were more in accord with the spirit of rehabilitation and preventive deterrence than with the spirit of retribution. (Braithwaite 1982, 1984; Braithwaite and Fisse 1983, 1985; Kadish 1963; Thomas 1982). These practices could be revived and applied to corporations. Fisse and Braithwaite (1983, 246) put it well: "If we are serious about controlling corporate crime, the first priority should be to create a culture in which corporate crime is not tolerated. The informal processes of shaming unwanted conduct and of praising exemplary behaviour need to be emphasized." When corporations behave criminally or otherwise illegally, they could face:

- Publicity orders as a formal sanction, paid for by the corporation, to advertise their harm and wrongdoing.
- Formal publicity following trials to convey information to the public concerning corporate transgressions and the consequences of noncompliance with the judgements laid down.
- Pre-sentence or probation orders against offending corporations, requiring disclosure of organizational reforms and disciplinary action undertaken as a result of the transgression.
- Mandatory corporate disclosure of risks of serious harm.

- Official government inquiries into corporate reactions to scandal, particularly those involving changes in corporate policies.
- National exposure of unacceptable corporate practices through the establishment of consumer information networks, investigative journalism networks, and complaint boards.
- The publication of corporation names in a government journal that catalogues all major actions against large corporations and is distributed free of charge to government departments, legislators, newspapers, media executives, educators, public interest groups and other interested parties.

In addition, contempt laws and rules of standing for investigative reporters could be liberalized to allow good-faith press comments on matters before the courts. Immunities from prosecution could be encouraged for voluntary corporate disclosure and cooperation, and *qui tam* suits (allowing citizens to proceed by means of civil actions to secure financial redress) could be promoted for consumer groups, thus fostering private prosecutions and securing for victims the funds from fines on corporate criminals (Braithwaite 1989, 142-43; Fisse and Braithwaite 1983, 243, 312; Clinard and Yeager 1980, 319-22). These measures could be combined with "affirmative duty orders" compelling corporate executives to exercise reasonable care to discover, prevent and publicize acquisitive corporate crime within the area of business under their effective control or to face penalty and sanction (Dershowitz 1968, 150).

Corporations should pay for publicizing their own misconduct, negligence, indifference, incompetence and greed. The first practical step might be to choose chief executives as targets for shaming, because it is they who set the tone of criminogenic corporate cultures (Clinard 1983; Braithwaite 1984, 1989). After all, they are the publicity beneficiaries who get their photographs in the business magazines and in the media. Accordingly, advertisements could take the following form: **WARNING: THE ILLEGAL DISPOSAL OF TOXIC WASTE WILL RESULT IN JAIL. WE KNOW. WE GOT CAUGHT! MULRONEY'S DISPOSAL COMPANY.** They might also include a letter paid for by the offending corporation, outlining the offense and the penalty and persuading the general public of the merits of environmental protection. Alternatively, crime control could be affected through regular "mug shots" of convicted corporate offenders published in the pages of *Fortune* or *Business Week* or, more significantly, in the daily press. In either case, they would take the form of imaginative writings directed at publicizing corporate harm and wrongdoing and butressing the legitimacy of communitarian concern and control.

Positive sanctions could also be used to counterbalance an increased use of shaming strategies, to help regulators maintain the good will of industry. Environmental protection awards, health and safety awards, consumer safety awards and so on might be made to qualifying corporations that accelerate beyond their "cleanup" timetables or come up with innovative health and safety measures (Stone 1975, 243; Braithwaite 1984, 304-5). Preference in government contracts, tax benefits, awards of merit and the like also could be made part of a proactive state program designed to publicize and reward corporate respect for the law (Clinard and Yeager 1980, 318).

The idea of strategic shaming for corporations has already been tried in some American industries, and the results have been inconclusive. Federal Trade Commission actions against STP (a marketer of oil additives for automotive products) to correct false, misleading and fraudulent advertising claims, and newspaper reporting of price-fixing in the heavy electrical industry and in the folding-carton industry cases resulted in "little negative publicity associated with corporate deviance" for shaming to be an effective control (Ermann and Lundman 1982, 144). However, the regulatory agencies were much too liberal in allowing the companies to advertise their wrongdoing in journals of corporate choice. They did not think the sanction of shame and positive repentance through to its logical conclusion. Potential consumers remained misled and cheated while other consumers learned of products they were not interested in and unwilling to buy. Implementation rather than the principle was at fault. As Box (1983, 68) notes, "that STP deliberately chose to place the correct information in obscure papers read by financial enthusiasts rather than moral enthusiasts . . . indicates just how much of a deterrent positive repentence could be if properly executed." Effective corporate shaming cannot be laissez faire. It must be state initiated, and monitored and ultimately authoritative.

We should not be naive about the possibilities of "strategic shaming." It works best in countries with strong communitarian cultures such as Japan or in smaller social units such as the family (Braithwaite 1989, 133-38). So will it work for corporations? Clinard (1983); Braithwaite (1984, 1989), Fisse and Braithwaite (1983) and Scholz (1984) say yes, under certain circumstances. First, it must be denunciatory and aim at promoting the role of conscience and social responsibility in legal compliance. The *moral* content of shaming and repentence must be accentuated for social control to work. "If there is no morality about the law, if it is just a game of national economic trade-offs, cheating will be rife" (Braithwaite 1989, 142).

Second, shaming must aim to reintegrate the corporation with the wider community so that informal social control from outside can penetrate the walls and corridors of corporate power. Shame should be used to internalize a commitment to the rules, while avoiding the pitfalls of systematic stigmatization. Securing compliance, in the first instance, should minimize punitive, adversarial approaches. Shaming strategies should eschew uncompromising, uniform and consistent punishment of corporate criminals and avoid establishing subcultures of regulatory resistance (Braithwaite 1982, 1991). The implication is that informal expressions of disapproval and anger, and reasoning about the harm and wrongdoing, can result in a corporate commitment to follow the rule of law or in an agreement to try harder for compliance in the future. Give talk a chance! But also provide "direct expressions of forgiveness and reconciliation to the offenders, proferring a repentant role, [and] punishment that maintains bonds of respect between enforcer and offender that invites the offender to accept its justice" (Braithwaite 1989, 140).

Third, strategic shaming must aim to overcome concerted corporate ignorance and to integrate internally fissured corporate structures. As we have seen, corporate harm, violence and theft flourishes best in organizations that divide and isolate people into sealed domains of knowledge and social responsibility. Concerted ignorance means that corporate executives can get away with "claiming not to know what is going on" in their business, with limiting moral and ethical responsibilities to others, and with incorporating scapegoat positions such as "vice-presidents responsible for going to jail." Crime will be controlled in corporate conglomerates where and when "shady individuals and crooked sub-units are exposed to shame by a responsible majority in the organization. Even if the majority are less than responsible, exposure gives maximum scope to such pangs of conscience . . . and increases vulnerability to control from without" (ibid., 145). The image is that of an organization "full of antennas," diligently regulating itself. Let a little shame shine in by mandating free and open channels to the top of the corporate bureaucracy and by implementing sound auditing and violation reporting policies that undercut introspective ignorance and foster mutual obligation, accountability and trust (Braithwaite 1979a, 1989, 145-48).

Fourth, strategic shaming must be accompanied with a resolve to "devolve responsibility for social control to agents who are in day-to-day relationships of interdependency with those to be regulated" (Braithwaite 1989, 149). This requires a compliance system structured along local industry lines. Thus, effective occupational health and safety regulation, for example, would involve recruiting "elected employee health and safety representatives in each workplace, as well as employer safety officers, to do most of the inspection and most of the enforcement" (ibid.,

149). Companies would be required to file and have approved their proposals for self-policing pollution, worker safety, product safety, etc. There would be strict standards and monitoring. Inspectors would be hired and paid for by the corporations and would therefore be insiders, not outsiders as regulatory agencies are currently. There would be better information access and flow, less antagonism and easier management. Each firm could tailor its rules within an overall program of state supervision. Management would not be allowed to overrule the inspectorate and public reporting and accountability would be persistent and rigorous (Braithwaite 1982). The role of the state is that of guardian, auditor and monitor. State regulation is at a distance and as a last resort.

Finally, strategic shaming is not a program devoid of formal punishment. Nor is it non-state-interventionist. Though persuasion is preferred, it is only rendered effective as a control strategy because it is underwritten by a process of punishment. The role of the state then is to forcefully intervene when community control and conscience fail, and to select the most serious cases of corporate crime for formal public punishment. The state should express the moral education functions of criminal law and dramatize the legitimacy of communal controls by showing that it backs up communal sanctions with severe deterrence if necessary. More state, shame-based punishment, not less, is needed. Feinberg (1970, 101-5) long ago observed that symbolic condemnation, coupled with harsher aspects of punishment, allows for authoritative disavowal of corporate illegality, reaffirmation of legal rules, moral reprobation and the absolution of innocent victims. Paradoxically, stigma, adverse publicity and other moral and legal disincentives now more than ever are needed to break down criminal corporate conduct and build the consciences and behavioural restraints that will allow organizational crime control to work by "interdependent monitoring within moral relationships" (Braithwaite 1989, 150-51).

Ultimately, strategic shaming is directed at the reputation of the firm and of corporate executives. It seeks to denounce the social value, competence, and social responsibility of a corporation for the death, harm and cost it has caused. The goal is not outcasting or fear mongering about formal punishment but the eventual atonement and reintegration of the corporate offender. The preventive effect of reintegratively shaming corporate criminals occurs when the offenders recognize the wrongdoing and shame themselves. Thus, in Katz's (1988, 27) words, they "become ashamed" of themselves, but they do not "become humiliated" of themselves. Reparation, not "just deserts," is the underlying principle. Shaming entails a "direct action model" rather than a "judiciary model." Its strategists are suspicious of criminal prosecution and they prefer a *process* of penality. Apprehension, publicity, confessions, reparation and reconciliation should all be tried before civil, legal or criminal remedies are considered. The virtues of shaming and positive repentence are its moral uprightness, its simplicity and its flexibility. It works, or could be made to work, best in cases where corporations wanted to avoid or to undo damages to their respectability.

There are, however, problems with this policy proposal. First, the company may refuse or not be deterred by the offer of repentence or the shame of bad publicity. This is as likely as not, and it is unclear as to why the community would succeed where the courts have not, especially when it involves individuals and organizations that are "one-shooters," as opposed to "repeat players" (Galanter 1974). After all, illegal profits may be worth a public black eye.

Second, even under shaming or cooperative regulation measures, the state may be able to impose a fine in response to noncompliance but, as we have seen, this normally would be small and inconsequential.

Third, criminal prosecution, though admittedly difficult, costly and ineffectual, is still the heaviest moral sanction a society can employ. It need not be abandoned or necessarily associated with regulatory failure (Coffee 1981; Shapiro 1985; Yoder 1978). It might become the basis for a more enlightened and effective crime control policy — one that the corporate sector will take seriously. Prosecution and conviction of corporations may be revitalized. As Cullen, Maakestad and Cavender (1987, 351) put it, "Corporations dó not appear to be invincible offenders. . . . Sanctions directed against corporate entities may play a meaningful role in deterring waywardness in the business community."

Fourth, the attachment of earnings from the illegal accumulation of capital may be a more effective deterrent than shame and social denunciation. A focus on nonfinancial matters such as good repute and corporate morale may have the potential to curb the energy of the aggressive executive and to help restructure career interests in favour of greater legal compliance, but a direct attack on the business objectives of sales, markets, earnings, property rights, and profits may be equally well placed.

Finally, models of positive repentance and reintegration underestimate the key role that corporate power plays in shaping the entire regulatory process. As we have seen, the state does not have a direct, unproblematic interest in achieving effective control of corporate crime, nor does it have the ability and necessary resources to achieve this goal. Yet existing talent and resources ought not be depleted further. Controlling corporate crime requires strategies that weaken the power of the corporate sector overall, while simultaneously strengthening the power of those organizing against corporate crime (Snider 1990, 21; Sargent 1990). This requires an interventionist, not a minimal, state. Powers and duties to interfere with private capital interests therefore need to be expanded and bolstered. State administrative agencies require laws that encourage flexibility but also permit greater bargaining and enforcement capacity. As Winter (1985, 240-41) recognizes:

> If legal doctrine allowed clear cut rules to be discarded whenever an agency preferred non-enforcement, the value of the legal rule as a bargaining chip would be diminished, for the regulatory process would begin with the assumption that full enforcement was not even a benchmark.

We know that the calculated loopholes of the law; the complexity of company records; problems in document access, retrieval and analysis; the burdens of legal proof "beyond a reasonable doubt"; and the difficulties of tracing corporate wrongdoing from one subsidiary to another and across national boundaries create major, costly obstacles to the criminal prosecution and conviction of corporations and their officials. Serious thought should be given to changing existing judicial principles in order to make them more effective against corporate crime. Foremost should be:

- Abandon the "right to trial by jury" and replace it with trials heard by a panel of judges or expert juries able to understand the complexities and specialisms of cases against corporations (Kadish 1963, 399; Braithwaite 1979b, 132; 1984, 311-14). These bodies should be publically operated administrative tribunals or commissions and so less bound to legal precedents and procedural constraints and more able to overcome some of the problems of excessive legal codification (Ball and Friedman 1968, 422-23).
- Strengthen regulatory agencies, especially in their legal departments, so as to develop a network of state lawyers sufficiently trained and experienced to combat, on equal terms, the abilities of corporate lawyers (Coleman 1989, 250; Conklin 1977, 145; Clinard and Yeager 1980, 315-16).
- Expand the limited intrusion of strict liability in criminal law to cover more and more corporate behaviour, thus obviating the need to show intent and responsibility and strengthening the more pressing need to compensate victims and make the offending corporation pay the price of justice (Conklin 1977, 143; Braithwaite 1984; Kadish 1963; Reasons 1982).

- Calibrate the law so it targets legal responsibility for decisions, policy implementation and results on key corporate officers and holds them responsible for corporate harm and wrongdoing and liable to criminal conviction (Conklin 1977, 143; Clinard and Yeager 1980, 318; Ermann and Lundman 1982, 169-74).
- Encourage class action suits allowing victims of corporate crime to join together and sue the offending corporation jointly. This is not only more economical but a valuable tool for consumer education and for legal mobilization against corporate violators (Conklin 1977, 135; Braithwaite 1984, 346-48).
- Transform the onerous burden of proof from "beyond reasonable doubt" to the "balance of probabilities" as it is under civil law. The test of accountability would be based on what an individual had knowledge of or reason to know and failed to act upon rather than authorized, ordered or acted upon. In other words it would be reasonable to ascribe criminal intent to a corporate executive who says: "I want the job done, but I don't want to know how you do it" (Braithwaite 1984, 323); also see Kadish 1963, 395; Levi 1984, 330-31; Dershowitz 1968, 150-53).
- Since the essence of corporate crime is not the behaviour of individuals but the behaviour of corporations, fixing criminal liability upon the corporation itself is vital. The level of intervention has to be organizational. Corporations and executives both should be prosecuted, but resources should be concentrated on the corporation for reasons of ability to pay fines and recompense victims, and because it recognizes the principle and prevention of collective wrongs and harms (Box 1983, 70; Conklin 1977, 144; Braithwaite,1984, 326-28; Kadish 1963, 395).
- Establish a corporate crime Act and a corporate crime index similar to the Criminal Code and Uniform Crime Index. Among other things, it would make it a felony for a corporation to conceal any product or process that might cause death or injury. A statute prohibiting "reckless employing" would require employers to prove that they are taking every reasonable measure to prevent harm, rather than the reversed onus of proof now used. And it would make it a crime to retaliate against citizens seeking to inform the public about such activities. The legislation would require corporations to provide workers, consumers, and the public with all available information about any hazards their activities may create. The corporate crime Act should be as concise and clear as possible to

reduce the existing and exhausting "cat and mouse approach" to legal contestation and loopholes (Conklin 1977, 141-42); Simon and Eitzen 1986, 267; Coleman 1989, 253; Braithwaite 1984, 343-44, 313-16; Geis 1973, 191; Snider 1991).

- Revise the terms of the "no contest" plea, which is frequently used and allows corporate offenders to escape the full impact of criminal sanctions and avoid paying civil damages to victims. At the very least, the law should allow the introduction of the "no contest" plea into civil proceedings as equivalent to a finding of guilt (Conklin 1977, 142).

It might be thought that these suggested changes amount to creating the beginnings of a parallel system of justice. We saw earlier that various protective judicial principles were established to safeguard the accused individual from a too powerful accusing state. The purpose was to establish, at least formally, a level playing field whereby individuals would not be unfairly convicted. But what about corporations? Should they enjoy the same constitutional benefits as individual citizens? I think not. It is clear from the above discussion that corporate power is considerable and that transnational corporations are more than a match for national state regulatory bodies. Corporations are neither financially weak nor politically powerless individuals. They are not about to be crushed by the prosecutory might of the state. On the contrary, corporations have shown themselves adept at taking advantage of laws that originally were intended to protect the weak (Cullen, Maakestad and Cavender 1987).

The rules surrounding rights to privacy, double jeopardy and harrassment and reasonable doubt should all be relaxed in cases where corporations are defendants (Braithwaite 1984, 339-43). After all, corporations can neither be imprisoned nor executed. Of course, in instances where the prosecution of individual corporate officials under statutes permitting the sanction of imprisonment occurs, then those defendants should be accorded the safeguards of criminal law. For lesser sanctions, these extreme protections need not apply to the same degree. It is unjustified and plainly biased to continue to strengthen the hand of corporate power by permitting and extending to them judicial privileges originally formulated to protect relatively powerless individuals (Cullen, Maakestad and Cavender 1987, 323). "The more the rich and the poor are dealt with according to the same legal propositions, the more the advantage of the rich is insured" (Braithwaite 1984, 342).

But more than different judicial principles and more organizational approaches to the issue are required. Two problems remain vexing: the low rate of detection and the inadequate record of penality. The state's chance of securing conviction is dependent upon a vigilant enforcement regime. We have noted the character of regulatory corporate crime management and found it wanting and defective in its ability to locate and process corporate offenders. The discovery of corporate crime has been most uncertain and irregular, relying, as most state agencies do, upon inadequate, inconstant, notified and often short and superficial inspections, or upon already "cooked" corporate data. Regulatory work is not as reactive as police work, but neither is it particularly proactive. Opening up the relatively sealed world of corporate crime may require more self-regulation and a reliance upon cooperative inside personnel, as shaming strategists say, but it will also be necessary to deploy a more compelling set of enforcement strategies. As Scott (1989, 582) notes , "Certainty or the probability of detection may be a more critical deterrent than a sentence because those persons may be particularly responsive to stigma." Chief among these enforcement strategies would be the following:

- The extensive use of undercover investigators, "sting" operations and electronic surveillance to infiltrate, detect, expose and prosecute corporate criminals and criminal corporations (Geis 1973, 192, and 1984; Box 1983, 74; Coleman 1989, 252; Scott 1989, 581-83).
- The encouragement of a public role in the control of corporate crime by providing mandatory disclosure rules, immunity and other financial incentives to hunt down corporate criminals inside corporate bureaucracies (Geis 1973, 192; Simon and Eitzen 1986, 267).
- The fostering of a "Workers Bill of Rights" and a "Whistle Blowing Protection Act" which prevents employer intimidation of workers for exercising their constitutional rights to freedom of expression, equal rights or privacy and which encourages and, in some cases, requires the reporting of corporate law violations (Braithwaite 1984, 343-44; Simon and Eitzen 1986, 267; Coleman 1989, 254).
- The promotion of the private policing of corporate crime through the use of state rewards, the promotion of *qui tam* actions (allowing citizens to collect fines, penalties or forfeitures by means of civil action for successful convictions) and the establishing of a corporate crime control marketplace for "business exploitation" (Simon and Eitzen 1986, 267-69; Miller 1973 208; Conklin 1977, 134).

- The cultivation of proactive victimization programs that encourage complaints and action from private individuals, public interest groups, and corporate competitors who have been victimized (Scott 1989).
- The strengthening of existing regulatory agencies by increasing staff and budgets to investigate, research, administer and prosecute corporate crime. Funding at ten times current levels would not be out of line with the importance of the problem and with the need for certainty of detection as a key element of deterrence. Expenditures such as these should, where possible, be paid out of a special corporate crime fine fund run by the state. Corporate wrongdoing and harm should pay for the cost of corporate surveillance, investigation and prosecution (Coleman 1989, 250; Scott 1989, 582; Clinard and Yeager 1980, 316).

Unlike the conventional offenders, business criminals are difficult to locate. Their victims, whether individuals or communities, need more efficient means of apprehending offending corporations. For their sakes and for those that follow, corporate informers, defectors, informants, complainants, and private corporate crime investigators are defensible, however much one might doubt their utility in the pursuit of conventional crime. Are stiffer penalties also needed along with widened judicial principles and more proactive policing?

Fines could certainly be raised above their current level, and some change has occurred in this regard. More, however, needs to be done. Perhaps fines should be assessed according to the nature of the violation and in accordance with corporate assets or profits rather than upon some fixed tariff (Clinard and Yeager 1980, 316; Conklin 1977, 138; Ermann and Lundman 1982, 144-50). Dershowitz (1968, 743) proposes "a *percentage fine* . . . whereby the maximum fine . . . imposed upon any corporation would be based upon the economic size of that corporation calculated from . . . the defendant corporation's taxable income or total capital." Criminal fines should be a profit-diminishing sanction as well as a criminal penalty. Far too often criminal fines do not pose a credible deterrent. Laws should be rewritten to require the convicted corporation to automatically pay a penalty equal to or larger than the amount of illegal profit. Where repeat offenders or violent offenses are involved, much stiffer financial penalties might be imposed, perhaps based on previous record, severity of damage and injury and the number of deaths the corporation caused (Coleman 1989, 251). Corporations should be the focus of criminal fines, and strict limits should be put on the transferability of fines. Insurance companies ought not to be allowed to bear the costs of fines through indemnity schemes for civil or criminal liability. Indeed, a condition of insurance coverage to corporations should be that firms possess adequate internal compliance systems and effective systems for reporting wrongdoing (Braithwaite 1984, 332; Simon and Eitzen 1986, 267; Stone 1975, 133-260).

Though fines are a relatively cheap and efficient form of sanction compared to imprisonment, they can be a crude instrument. Coffee (1981) has suggested the "equity fine" as an innovative sanction on corporate crime. Under this form of "capitalist punishment," the guilty corporation must issue new equity securities to the value of the fine. The securities, in turn, are transferred to a government crime victim compensation fund. For example, if the corporation had one million shares outstanding, a 10 percent equity fine would see 100,000 shares handed over to the victim compensation fund. The value of an equity fine is as follows: (a) it imposes large penalties without depleting the capital of the corporation, (b) it does not have a spillover of sanctions onto innocent employees, creditors and suppliers, (c) it strikes at the privileges of senior management who generally have high amounts of shares in the corporation and (d) it frightens investors away from legally risky companies. Combined with high negative publicity, the equity fine is a criminal sanction, an attachment on illegal profits and earnings, and a way of restituting victims (Braithwaite 1984, 335).

Fines on individual corporate offenders should also be increased and used more extensively and innovatively. Unscrupulous executives ought not to be free from criminal liability or penalty, or have the corporation and its stockholders pay the charge for their recklessness and harm. As Geis (1973, 191) notes, "criminal prosecution of a corporation is rather ineffective unless one or more of the individual officers is also proceeded against." Accordingly, fines should be substantial, taking into account the offenders' earnings and assets and the harm and damage done. Fining and shaming might be combined. Deterrence could be made more effective if financial loss is significant and if it is accompanied with loss of individual prestige, decline in corporate worth, job dissatisfaction and humiliation in the witness box (Fisse and Braithwaite 1983, 243). The process as well as the loss of income is the punishment!

More and larger fines enforced through civil procedures might also ably serve to deter corporate crime (*Harvard Law Review* 1979, 1375), attach illegal profits (Dershowitz 1968,144) and compensate victims of corporate crime (Cullen, Maakestad and Cavender 1987). Civil remedies are, however, difficult to win partly because corporations are more powerful and more skilled in this type of litigation and partly because the rules of damage suits showing prior criminal conviction and proving with certainty a "direct and proximate" causal relationship between violation and damages are heavy obligations to demonstrate. Dershowitz (1968, 144, 148) and Conklin (1977) suggest that a modified and private single damage system be implemented that would allow for awards of "any sum between actual and treble damages" and eliminate the use of the "no contest" plea in criminal cases as an impediment to civil cost recovery. They propose a "civil attachment proceeding" to recover illegal gains and allow government to combine a criminal course of action with an essentially civil remedy. It would work as follows:

> Prior to the filing of the government action, any allegedly damaged plaintiff could sue for compensation. . . . If the government prevailed in its action and the defendant corporation's illegal profits were attached, any person (or corporation) who . . . had a damage remedy against the defendant corporation could seek compensation by filing an action against the government. . . . If at the end of the period of limitations the face amount of the total claims did not exceed the attached profits, the government could . . . settle all claims which it felt were justified . . . if, however, the face amount of claims exceeded the attached profits, the government could not enter into any settlement without the consent of the defendant corporation. . . . The defendant corporation would be permitted to defend . . . against any claim it felt was spurious. But if all the attached profits were distributed . . . claimants remaining uncompensated would be permitted to sue the defendant corporation directly (Dershowitz 1968, 144).

Such changes would decrease legal delays and unfavourable plea bargaining and increase the number of civil trials for business crime and the number of private damage suit awards. The educative effect of these fining sanctions might very well be new moral boundaries regarding corporate harm, violence, damage and death. The key, of course, is to find the balance between a reasonable fining option and one that cripples. The proper moral economy of fining must achieve justice without bankrupting corporations and displacing innocent employees, consumers and dependants (Box 1983, 71; Coleman 1989, 252; Braithwaite 1984, 351-52). It must also signal to investors and stockholders that the price of illegal enrichment is a substantial burden if they invest in business crime or criminal corporations. Then, perhaps, sanctions against corporate crime "can be built into the very structure of the marketplace itself" (Geis 1973, 194).

Corporations cannot be put in jail, but individual corporate executives may be sentenced to varying terms of imprisonment. Knowledgeable criminologists and sociologists are calling for more extensive use of prisons and for longer sentences. Glassbeek and Rowland (1979) have developed detailed legal arguments as to why corporate killing and harm at work should be treated as typical crimes of violence. Pearce and Tombs (1990, 439) state that motoring offences, which are criminally sanctioned, are similar in many ways to offences committed by corporations, and they conclude that it is "only the fear of effective legal sanctions that will make management genuinely safety-conscious". Clinard and Yeager (1980, 317) say "a mandatory six month's sentence for most offenses or a minimum sentence of 18 months for serious violations should be provided by law." Cullen and Dubeck (1985) argue that sanctioning the corporation is the most prudent and equitable policy. Prison carries with it an enormous moral stigma and it may be used to educate as well as to punish criminals. The arguments for severe punishment are several. First, it incapacitates corporate offenders temporarily so they cannot victimize employees, consumers, communities, other corporations or shareholders. Second, corporate criminals are more readily deterred by the threat of imprisonment. They fear it as a sanction and have more to lose, and so this fear will lead to a welcome improvement in their conduct. Third, jail terms will deter others. The example of a prominent corporate executive imprisoned for five to ten years would act as a powerful deterrent to other corporate offenders. It might also spur investors to monitor their management teams more closely. Fourth, imprisonment is fair and redresses imbalances. Greater overall equity is achieved by imprisoning the powerful, since it is the powerless offender who is most frequently jailed. Finally, the expression of condemnation in the form of incarceration allows the state to register disapprobation of corporate crime on behalf of its citizens (Cullen, Maakestad and Cavender 1987, 344; Geis 1973, 195-97; Conklin 1977, 138; Coleman 1989, 252; Von Hirsch 1985, 53).

Imprisoning executives might, through incapacitation and deterrence, therefore lower the incidence of corporate crime. But as Box (1983, 71), Ward (1986) and Braithwaite (1984, 328-30; 1990) note, this may be a tentative and overly optimistic conclusion. Prisons are also costly, and dehumanizing insitutions that often return people who are worse liabilities to society than when they entered. Moreover, if corporations routinely promote or recruit new personnel to replace the imprisoned or reluctant, then scaring executives and removing them to jail may have only a small consequence on corporate crime. Finally, courts have been very unwilling to relax procedural safeguards that make it difficult to prosecute corporate crime when loss of liberty through incarceration is at issue. When fines or other penalties are involved, the courts have been more liberal in what they have allowed (*Harvard Law Review* 1979, 1306-7). This makes a strong case for selective use of imprisonment provisions for most corporate crime statutes. More detection and certainty may bring more deterrence for the dollar than "just deserts" (Braithwaite 1984, 330; Conklin 1977, 139).

However, other "prison-like" strategies could be used. Instead of serving time in prison, convicted corporate executives could serve a "term of disqualification." The convicted violator might be barred from assuming similar management positions within the corporation or in another corporation for a five-year period (Clinard and Yeager 1980, 318; McDermott 1982, 604-61). As Geis (1973, 194) observes, "Why put the fox immediately back in charge of the chicken coop?" A forced retirement for reasons of corporate crime does not seem to be an unreasonable imposition. This might be followed by a "term of atonement" when, for a year or more, corporate offenders would be required to make public repentance at private cost for crimes committed. This would include lecturing to business, community, professional and educational groups and working with government agencies in the fight against corporate crime (ibid., 191-92; Braithwaite 1990). It might be thought of as a "halfway measure" towards offender reintegration. Disqualification may also be aimed at the corporation itself. A system of penalty points similar to those contained in motor vehicle regulations could be applied by factory inspectorates, resulting in automatic fines and on-the-spot imposition of penalty points. As with driving offenses, recalcitrant offenders could be sanctioned by having their company disqualified temporarily after reaching a certain number of points. Thus court cases would be largely unnecessary for a whole range of corporate violations (Hadden 1983; Pearce and Tombs 1990).

"Imprisonment" of all or part of the offending corporation by means of nationalization or divestiture may be another means to achieve maximal impact on corporate crime. By deconcentrating and divesting corporations of certain product lines or subsidiaries (depending of course on the type and severity of the offense), and by placing publicly-appointed directors to oversee the process, the chances of recidivation could be reduced substantially. Corporations would be compelled to restructure, to break up into smaller units and to forfeit some of their assets and profits to the state (Clinard and Yeager 1980; Dershowitz 1968; Simon and Eitzen 1986). In turn, these assets may be sold or run as businesses with employees, consumers and the public being the primary beneficiaries. For example, if a corporation is convicted, part of its sentence might be to divest itself of a subsidiary worth $100 million. The monies could then be used to compensate corporate crime victims or be invested in a community business run by a democratically elected board of directors. Similarly, nationalization for a specific period (length depending upon severity of the offense and time required for rehabilitation) might be a just measure of pain for corporations that are criminally out of control. What is at stake now is no trifling fine, but real and substantial assets and profits, as well as control and management of the corporation (Box 1983,72; Braithwaite and Geis 1982, 300-305).

However, within the current political and economic climate of Canada, the United States and Great Britain, such sanctions might seem severe or inappropriate. The argument against them would be that jobs will be lost, firms will go under, efficiency will be sacrificed and prices will rise. As Snider (1991, 214) observes, governments are "wary of offending capital, since they have little direct control over it and it is typically fluid." They are reluctant to impose restrictions, obligations or stringent regulations because they fear that such measures will "frighten off the much sought-after investment, and engender the equally dreaded loss" of political credibility.

These arguments may not be dismissed easily. There would be costs to deconcentration, divestiture and public ownership, although corporate capital has largely exaggerated them. But, then again, there is also the cost of *not* divesting, deconcentrating and nationalizing — corporate killing and harm, community destruction, and environmental pollution to say nothing of economic inequality, higher prices, regional imbalances and global war (Box 1983, 72-73).

Nevertheless, a number of other measures would achieve the same limited objectives. They are of two types: interventionist court orders and administrative remedies.

The courts could impose probation order conditions on corporate offenders compelling them to "clean up" their organizational act (Fisse and Braithwaite 1983, 243, 312). Courts would appoint teams of probation officers under the supervision of an auditor or other relevant expert (i.e., in pollution control, quality control, etc.) drawn from a network of lawyers, social scientists, accountants, engineers, chemists, etc., selected to meet case requirements. The purpose of the probation team would be to monitor standard procedures, internal compliance systems, accounts, research and testing programs, data reporting systems, communications and authority structures and any other organizational dimensions that might be associated with a convicted corporation's criminal conduct and then to report, recommend and ensure that an order to restructure has been carried out under pain of revoking the probation order and returning to court for further sentencing (Coffee 1980; Braithwaite 1984, 338; Box 1983, 72). In order to defray the increased cost of the probation service, the offending corporation would be charged for the full cost of the implementation of the probation order.

Alternatively, the courts or regulatory agencies might issue "consent decrees" or withhold sentencing until the convicted corporation has taken stock of its organizational problems and implemented acceptable remedial action. Then, if not satisfied they could impose an interventionist court order (Clinard 1979, 30; Thomas 1982, 118-19; Braithwaite 1984, 339). Once again, the previous record of offenses and the seriousness of the crime would be crucial in determining a course of action. Probation would not mean a lesser penalty or an occasional visit to a local probation office for a convivial chat. It would be instead a sequestration of a portion of the corporate structure, followed by shaming and penalty, however temporary.

Another possibility is that the court could impose a "community service charge" upon the corporation. Under this arrangement, a business could be required to, for example, repair damaged community property and clean up environmental pollution, build new institutions such as hospitals and schools and pay for roads, bridges, sewers, community centres, day care facilities, libraries and the like. The exact service charges would be tailored to the nature of the offense. Thus a company found guilty of manslaughter and/or criminally negligent homicide involving its own workforce could be sentenced to a community service charge directing them to build a public athletic center in the victim's name or it could be forced to forsake some of its profits or sell some of its products at strictly cost price to those who have been injured or are in need of subsidy (Box 1983, 73; Geis 1973, 194, and 1984).

A final interventionist measure might be to act forcefully on behalf of victims and direct corporations to compensate them. If we are to take seriously the claim that "an ideology which cuts corporations off from obligations to the community is criminogenic" (Braithwaite 1989, 144), then the courts should move, under criminal jurisdiction, to award compensatory damages. This would avoid lengthy, costly and difficult-to-win civil actions. One possible solution would be the establishment of "no-fault compensation funds" for victims of defective consumer products such as drugs, automobiles, housing and the like. Victims could claim damages without having to prove corporate criminal intent or negligence before receiving compensation (Braithwaite 1984, 344). The fund could be government-sponsored and run like an insurance fund but financed from mandatory corporate contributions. Developments in the United States, Europe and Japan towards "no blame" consumer policies and stricter product liability plans minimally strengthen the victim's hand while slightly weakening the legal power of the corporate giants. These victim compensation schemes easily could be extended to cover other types of corporate injury and loss, in line with the principle of "repairing" damages done (ibid., 344-45; Box 1983, 74).

New administrative remedies might also be used to control corporate crime. They are many, and so I shall discuss only the major ones:

- Corporate accountability to both investors and the public could be increased through a unified federal government chartering system. Under this arrangement:

    1. corporations whose gross assets (including those of subsidiaries) exceeded a set amount, say $200,000, would be required to obtain a federal license to do inter-state, interprovincial and international business.
    2. Detailed reporting on the financial affairs of the corporation, including dealings with foreign firms, would be mandatory and would have to be forwarded on a regular basis to regulatory agencies and be made publically available.
    3. Any proposals to change corporate policy would require full disclosure of corporate operations, give stockholders the right to amend corporate by-laws and recall any director, provide more opportunities for stockholder nominations of board members, provide a full-time staff to the board of directors to monitor independently corporate procedures and compliance systems, and require a community impact evaluation when a corporation's plant is to be relocated.
    4. Directors may not be employed by or have a financial interest in a competitor but would be required to have a financial interest in their own corporation.
    5. Firms would be prohibited from acquiring the stocks, assets or property of another company, from granting or receiving any discrimination in price, service or allowances except in demonstrated cost-saving cases, from engaging in tie-in arrangements or exclusive dealerships and from participating in any system of interlocking control over any other corporation.
    6. Boards of chartered firms would be expanded to include worker and consumer representatives, and the corporations would be required to give the public much greater access to their records on things such as product safety research, dan-

gerous plant emissions, illegal activities of their subsidiaries or subunits, workers' health and safety conditions, and plans for factory closures.

7. Corporations would be "constitutionalized," giving employees rights on the job that they enjoy elsewhere as citizens: rights of free speech, assembly and privacy. Prohibited would be pre-employment lie detector tests, maintaining inaccessible or unchallengeable personnel files, and unjust dismissals.

8. Customers and communities would be protected by creating many competitive firms out of the very small number that now dominate most industries. Corporations with monopoly or semimonopoly holdings and power would be subdivided, whereas those seeking such power in the future would be prohibited from doing so.

9. Penalties would range from fines to actual revocation of licenses following hearings by regulatory agencies and actions instituted by the federal attorney general's office in the appropriate courts (Clinard and Yeager 1980, 310-13; Coleman 1989, 256; Nader et al. 1976; Ermann and Lundman 1982, 159-63; Simon and Eitzen 1986, 268-69).

- Corporations should be forced to develop better internal controls through the use of general public directors (GPDs), special public directors (SPDs) and through internal auditors and corporate ombudspersons. Under this proposal:

  1. Boards of Directors of large corporations would have to add, in varying numbers, permanent GPDs to their ranks. They would be selected and paid for by the general public through an appropriate federal commission while maintaining an office at corporate headquarters. Their activities would include making corporate leaders more aware of social issues, corporate crime, and the needs for new legislation, acting as conduits for "whistle-blowing" within the corporate bureaucracy and promoting public interest movements outside corporate walls.

  2. Boards of directors of large corporations would have to add in varying numbers and at varying times SPDs to their corporate inner circle. They would focus on specific problems and would be placed in corporations only when specific violations and crimes warranted. For example, the problems

associated with asbestos, waste, pollution, consumer safety, and nuclear energy meltdowns and leaks would require the appointment of an appropriately skilled SPD.

3. Those assigned with keeping the corporation compliant with the law must be given more organizational clout. Whether by means of new legislation, court order or self-regulation, compliance personnel must be upgraded and professionalized. An ombudsperson or administrative tribunal should be established to hear complaints. Reports would be made directly to the chief executive officer, thus tainting him or her with the knowledge of crime or potential crime. Corporate decisions about ethical, legal and criminal matters would be written down to create a kind of corporate case law. Auditors would also be encouraged to check on accounting procedures, report them to the highest level and so make it more difficult to conduct secret and illegal matters or claim innocence of criminality. Alternatively, auditors could be legally required to search out fraud and deception in corporate activities and to report them to enforcement agencies. Major corporations would be required to pay an audit fee to a government clearing house, which would then select the firm to do the actual audit (Braithwaite 1979b, 132, and 1984, 363-67; Coleman 1989, 253-57; Conklin 1977, 134-46; Ermann and Lundman 1982, 163-64; Simon and Eitzen 1986, 269).

• All corporate executives would be licensed to practice, just as members of other professional groups are. A condition of license would be legal and ethical worthiness. The main merit of the licensing system would be to create a mechanism for disbarring corporate offenders found guilty of ethical or legal obligations or of criminal wrongdoing (Conklin 1977, 145). Special publicly operated regulatory or administrative tribunals would be established to review and judge cases against individual executives. Considerations of social justice would outweigh considerations of strict law. As Coleman (1989, 253) notes, "if the evidence warranted, the hearing officer would be empowered to prohibit an offender from working for any major corporation for a fixed number of years. . . . Such a procedure would provide a means of sanctioning executives' misconduct without having to prove criminal intent." Public accountability of discretion thus would have priority over legal complexity, codification and corporate law manipulation (Braithwaite 1979b, 132; 1984, 311-19).

• The principle of licensing should be extended to cover broader areas of production, use, storage and distribution of dangerous products. Similar to Ministry of Transportation certificates for automobile use, corporations should be subjected, on a select basis, to independent certificating agencies, especially where their products or industry causes high health and environmental risks, e.g., chemical, nuclear and hazardous substance industries (Pearce and Tombs 1990, 435).

• Convicted corporations would have special public interest enforcement officers placed in corporate headquarters to represent the public's trust. Their task would be to assure that judgements against corporations are being implemented, laws are being complied with, mandated reforms are being put in place and environmental impacts of future actions by convicted corporations are examined and approved (Simon and Eitzen 1986, 267).

• Convicted corporations have an obligation to repay the harm and losses caused by their criminality. A government-run but privately financed mandatory replacement or referral system would reimburse victims of corporate crime (especially consumers) for economic losses brought about by illegal and dishonest dealings with corporate capital (Conklin 1977, 131; Simon and Eitzen 1986, 267).

There can be little doubt that these reforms have merit. The selective and more frequent use of fines, administrative measures, probation orders, community service charges, refund and compensation orders — particularly when coupled with law and enforcement reforms, strategic shaming for the corporation and increased and more severe imprisonment for corporate officials — would undoubtedly achieve the aims of deterrence, incapacitation, rehabilitation, and reparation and restitution better than the present system of lax regulation and enforcement, paltry fines and short imprisonment sentences. This list of strategic reforms may be thought of as a pyramidal package based on an implicit hierarchy of penalty.

Assuming that corporate self-regulation and self-surveillance has failed or is impossible, then the following course of action would be pursued. First, efforts would be made to persuade the corporation to comply, repair, restitute, and eventually reintegrate into a law-abiding path. Second, official warnings would be delivered, enjoining corporate conformity to the law. Informal processes of social control such as shaming, conscience-building, and even adverse publicity would be used. The appeal would be to the catalyzation of communitarian corporate controls, enlisting the corporation to accept the justice of the punishment. Third, compulsory civil charges leading to administrative and monetary penalties would be assessed should corporate recalcitrance continue unabated. This entails fines, forced injury compensation schemes, damage suits, probation orders, divestitures and possibly debarments. The final step would be to compulsory criminal indictment and prosecution, with sanctions ranging from criminal fines and prison sentences to removal of operating licences, deconcentration and plant shutdown. Regulators would intervene at each stage of the sequence of control and punishment. Their involvement would be mandatory and so would avoid exclusive reliance on civil and administrative penalties or criminal sanctions or on naive persuasion/education/self-regulation strategies (Braithwaite 1989, 124-86; Snider 1990; Vaughan 1983). But are these strategies enough and will they succeed?

• 6 •
A Social Movement
Against Corporate Crime

In their book *Corporate Crime Under Attack*, Cullen, Maakestad and Cavender (1987, x, 25, 78) observe that corporations are on the defensive and increasingly subject to the use of criminal law and penal sanctions. But they also conclude that the impact of legal prosecutions and sanctions "often has been more symbolic than real." There are reasons then for supposing that if the above modest reform proposals were adopted, they might only marginally reduce the scope and volume of corporate crime. This is not because these ideas are calculated to be ineffective or because regulators will be co-opted or unwilling to enforce laws. Nor are such proposal remedies "flaky," naive or idealistic. They could be made effective. Greater social control over the activity of corporations is a worthwhile but difficult goal to achieve.

There have been constructive engagements with the law, and capital has made and will have to continue to make concessions that run counter to its own economic interests (Sargent 1990; Snider 1987; Sumner 1981; Pearce and Tombs 1989). Regulatory reforms have been successful. Many rivers and streams are less polluted than they were twenty years ago, the lead has been removed from gasoline in most countries, many manufactured food products are now free of obvious toxins, new health and safety regulations have saved thousands of lives in factories, coal mines and homes, and consumer safety initiatives have reduced poisonings and deaths in the medical field (Fisse and Braithwaite 1983; Snider 1990, 1991; Claybrook 1984).

Criminalization, corporate organizational reform, publicity and sham-

ing, legal changes, alterations in the regulatory compliance and enforcement processes, and heavy penalties are not in themselves panaceas to
the problem of corporate crime, but they are strategic weapons brought
to bear upon capital as a social class. As Sumner (1981, 87-88) notes:
"Legal forms of resistance emerge alongside economic forms. . . . We
should support struggles which effectively remove the legal inequalities" between different social classes. Law in this sense mediates class
relations. It is not just an instrument of domination. It contains the
positive functions of civil resistance and rights struggle (Thompson 1977,
258-69; 1980, 153, 164-80). Brickey and Comack (1987, 103) put it well:
"Law is an arena of struggle." It is a product and object of people in
conflict and thus "rights discourse at the least offers the potential of
facilitating the mobilization of political action among subordinate groups"
(ibid.).

Legal reforms, however, have been most successful in deterring
smaller, nation-bound corporations and those whose capital equipment
is relatively fixed and who need local and more specialized labour forces.
Legal regulation also has been relatively effective in controlling insider
trading and stock market fraud (recent sensational scandals in the USA
and Canada notwithstanding) because this type of corporate crime
severely disrupts the interests of the corporate sector overall. Capital is
more willing to accept reforms that protect the sanctity of the investment
and accumulation markets and mechanisms, while governments are
more willing to regulate stock markets because they view them as a
necessity for a thriving private sector and for their own long-term fiscal
arrangements (Coleman 1989; Snider 1991). Laws have not, however,
been framed with a mind towards affecting the operations of transnational
capital in a strong imperialist core state, nor have they been especially
effective in protecting the environment or limiting trusts and monopolies
in the marketplace.

Thus, we must not overexaggerate the power and promise of law and
administrative reform. There are costs to focusing on civil and criminal
law first and foremost in the struggle against corporate crime. Constructive engagement with legal reform necessarily involves according legitimacy to legal codes and to the criminal justice system and its control over
the ways in which problems and politics get priorized. Victims of
corporate crime may rightly feel little direct empowerment and social
justice, and the orbit of state control may be extended and strengthened
in ways that exploit the socially marginalized while claiming to combat
the powerful (Snider 1987, 1991). Smart (1989, 144, 161) warns that law
may be an uncertain ally for social reform. Law's juridogenic nature leads
law to produce effects that "make conditions worse, and in worsening

conditions we make the mistake of assuming that we need to apply more doses of legislation." In areas such as rape and child sexual abuse, she states, the "legal 'cure' is frequently as bad as the original abuse." Radicals, she says, should concentrate on the law's power to define and disqualify the truth of events and should be wary of the law's capacity to reform. Moreover, backlashes do occur. Vogel (1986) reminds us that the environmental reforms of the 1970s caused a considerable corporate mobilization for deregulation that effectively stalled the cause of radical ecological reform. The unintended consequence of law reform, not for the first time, may very well be diversion, displacement, denial and subversion of corporate harm and wrongdoing.

The power of law is perhaps most uncertain when it comes to regulating the wayward giant transnational corporations. Many TNCs are so powerful that they can buy off provinces, states and entire nations. As Nader and Green (1973, 79) long ago observed, "General Motors could buy Delaware . . . if DuPont were willing to sell it." The same could be said about K.C. Irving and New Brunswick in Canada.

Outright law manipulation and violation are combined with law evasion strategies in cases involving TNCs. As Braithwaite (1984, 369) notes:

> If developed countries have tough laws to control the testing of experimental drugs on human beings, then the testing can be done in the third world. If one country bans a product, then stocks can be dumped in a more permissive country. . . . [There are] seemingly endless possibilities for international law evasion.

Working conditions, physical environments and consumer protections have all been taken advantage of by international capital. "Dirty industries" involving asbestos, arsenic and carcinogenics have been moved to Latin America. Health problems have been exported to countries in Southeast Asia where legal and medical protection is almost nonexistent. In other cases, TNCs have relocated polluting industries to less developed countries in order to circumvent environmental protection laws in their home nation. Hazardous waste products have been exported abroad as TNCs avoided the costs of mandated controls on waste storage. Shoddy and unsafe consumer products — the Dalkon Shield, children's sleepwear, dangerous drugs, harmful milk products — have been dumped on Third World markets after they have been found unsafe in First World countries.

Accordingly, some solutions will have to address the "space between national laws" and be international in substance. It may be that the laws of nation-states represent a "poor starting point" and a "theoretically inappropriate framework for the study of injurious" corporate crime, in which case the search for a more adequate framework must include transnational standards for evaluating the conduct of corporations (Michalowski and Kramer 1987, 40, 45). As Braithwaite (1979b, 140-44) notes, as long as "crime prevention planning remains fixed at the level of individuals as citizens of nation-states, control of the activities of transnational corporations as collective citizens of the international community will remain a pipe dream." New, broader political definitions of corporate transgressions need to be constructed. Organizations such as the United Nations, the Organization for Economic Cooperation, the International Labour Organization, the World Health Organization and a variety of intergovernmental working groups, commissions and councils are crucial to the evolution of worldwide sets of principles and definitions regarding corporate conduct. These organizations provide global arenas for social control activities: consumer protection, international safeguards against exposure to hazardous products, control over resources, and accountability for corporate wrongdoing, injury and death. International discourses, standards and censures should define and account for crimes that arise in a transnational context.

In this regard, the United Nations Code of Consumer Behaviour and Code of Corporate Conduct may be thought of as a new "set of international norms" that regulate the conduct of transnational business and around which corporate crime may be judged (Braithwaite 1984, Chapter 2). These codes promote respect for national sovereignty; human rights and freedoms; consumer, worker and environmental safety; and observance of domestic laws, regulations and administrative practices. And they forbid unfair business activities, bribery, corruption and interference in the practical affairs of duly elected governments. They represent legislated concepts of crime negotiated in a global context, carry considerable international moral stigma and move beyond the limits of national legal systems and the platitudinous codes of conduct adopted by international business organizations (Michalowski and Kramer 1987, 41-44). These codes and declarations of rights should be made as absolute as possible, recognizing that the obligations the codes impose on appropriate others to protect or promote those interests may not in all instances be categorical or fulfillable.

Yet more than an "adequate framework" is required. Ultimately, international solutions should include the following:

 • National legal standards should be internationally harmonized so lowest-common-denominator regulation can be transformed into highest-common-factor regulation. Harmonization need not be perfect, but it should seek to diminish the differences between national standards so as to remove the incentives of the international evasion game (Clinard and Yeager 1980, 325).

• Where possible and necessary, the lifting of standards may be accomplished most easily on a regional basis. Thus regional cooperation and networks may be sufficient to thwart transnational law evasion. Again the strategy would be to "up the ante" in one region of the world to discourage transnational relocation (Braithwaite 1979b, 1984, 1989; Michalowski and Kramer 1987).

• Efficient international communications about the adverse reactions caused by transnational corporate crime should be established. All too often either by neglect or design, hazards, dangers, harms and homicides are not communicated globally. Unsafe drugs are not reported by subsidiary firms to their parent organization or these reports fail to be passed on from one continent to another. Much "willful blindness" occurs. At minimum, what is required is (1) an international reporting system backed up with legal punishment for failure to report and (2) an international product and guarantee status document that provides up-to-date information on the status of the product: approvals, side effects, warnings, etc. (Braithwaite 1984, 370-71).

• Global enforcement should be coordinated and information about enforcement actions taken against transnationals should be exchanged internationally. As Braithwaite (1984, 374) notes, "Ultimately, international sanctioning methods are necessary to control activities which either fall between the cracks of national laws or spread one offence across a patchwork of national jurisdictions."

• Internationalization of consumerism, environmentalism and trade unionism needs to be promoted as countervailing forces against the internationalization of capital (Clinard and Yeager 1980, 323-24).

• International administrative tribunals, consumer information networks, investigative journalism networks and complaints boards to expose, publicize and adjudicate cases of transnational corporate crime should be established (Fisse and Braithwaite 1983, 243, 312; Michalowski and Kramer 1987; Simon and Eitzen 1986).

These worldwide measures, along with the administrative remedies mentioned in Chapter 5, might eliminate some of the pessimism about the regulation of transnational corporations. But they need to be backed up by nation-states. Supranational regulatory authorities are becoming stronger, but they still lack the clout and leverage that national governments possess. As Braithwaite (1984, 375) observes:

> National states have such bargaining tools — they set company taxes and tariffs, give investment allowances, influence the wage-determination process, approve products for heavy government subsidies and have control over many other allocative decisions which vitally affect the interests of transnational companies.... A supra-national regulatory authority would not even have the potential to use such bargaining implements.

The irony of the international control of transnational capital is that the best regulation regimes are still nation-based bodies, even though, as we have seen, national governments do not always use these tools very strategically to limit corporate crime.

Nation-states have been hard pressed to find the determination and imagination to combat the worst corporate offenders; maybe it will take international solutions to finally crack corporate crime. But these measures will not succeed where local ones have failed unless they are integrated into a broader movement to transform the institutional structure of corporate capitalism. As Barnett (1981, 23) has noted: "If we are to reduce production-related crime rather than merely redistribute its gains, we need to move away from either corporate or state capitalism."

Many of the reforms and remedies are admirable, but they should sharpen their aim at "the root cause of corporate crime: the system of political economy that makes crime both profitable and even necessary" (Simon and Eitzen 1986, 270). Legal, organizational and administrative reform efforts "must be coupled with wider political struggles" (Sargent 1990, 109). Symbolic politics must give way to a political movement against corporate crime that is actively committed to bringing about fundamental change in the political economy and quality of social life (Bowles, Gordon, and Weisskopf 1984).

The social movement against corporate crime requires not only strategies that weaken the power of the corporate sector, such as legal reforms, shaming, negative publicity, and the use of civil and criminal sanctions, but also strategies that simultaneously strengthen the power of oppositional social groups. Hills (1987, 201-3) observes that defining the solution to the corporate crime problem as primarily a question of legality and insufficient sanctions has the unfortunate effect of directing the focus of political action away from the organized struggles of consumers, environmentalists, workers and feminists, and towards the role of law and state enforcement regimes. A criminal justice focus may reinforce a negative victimology and a fatalistic political agenda. Individuals and communities are perceived as victims of capitalist greed and inadequate state intervention rather than as active political agents with claims, demands and rights. In his view, a broad-based social movement must anchor the attack against corporate crime and pilot a radical reform agenda.

> A necessary and crucial step is to educate the public to the horrendous consequences of corporate wrongdoing — the damaged human lives, disease-stricken bodies, and other illnesses and injuries inflicted on workers and consumers. Until there is greater public understanding of the relationship between corporate decision-making and human suffering, indeed, until there is a public sensibility that provides moral outrage at this corporate indifference, the far-reaching structural reforms that could make a major and lasting difference are unlikely to occur (ibid., 202).

Direct empowerment in the form of rights struggles is a promising second step for social change. Rights struggles are moral struggles of a fundamentally important kind. Following Lukes (1987, 67) we may define human rights as "strongly prima facie rights which, in general, are justified in defending people's vital interests and which, in general, override all other considerations bearing upon some policy or action, whether these concern goals and purposes or the protection of other, less central rights." In Dworkin's (1977) words, rights struggles have a "trumping" effect: to believe in them is to be committed to expanding and defending them. They entail a relationship of justice predicated on the premise of treating persons as ends and not merely as means. In turn, certain ways that persons, corporations or the state may use others are ruled out. Rights struggles thus create a link between absolute rights and pragmatic social policies. As Sumner (1981, 85) observes:

> It is very important to recognize the political value of having a prima facie presumption of right established in law. Rights are guidelines which strongly suggest to decision-makers that unless there is strong contrary right or statute they must make a particular type of decision, or risk moral and political calumny.

Turner (1986, 89-100), in his study of citizenship and capitalism, has shown that the historical emergence of political rights is the outcome of class struggles, egalitarian ideologies, and ethnic conflict, resistance and struggle. Social movements — whether promoted by trade unions, women's groups, the young, the elderly, environmentalists, etc. — have expanded the boundaries of citizenship. The first wave of citizenship rights reform undercut the formal role of property in the definition of citizen. The second wave removed sex from the definition of citizenship. The third wave of rights reform involved a redefinition of age and kinship ties within the family as a feature of citizenship. Recent social legislation on children and the aged, for example, may be regarded as part of the expanding agenda of claims for civil status in a time when property, sex and age barriers are collapsing as definitions of social membership. Finally, the last wave of citizenship rights has had the effect of ascribing rights to nature and the environment. The legal status of animals, and embryos and the protection of the natural world are now hotly contested social issues which indicates the outwardly expanding character of rights movements.

Fighting for rights, of course, is never finally finished nor is there a guaranteed outcome underpinning these struggles. The results of rights movements may be positive in that new rights are created or lost ones reaffirmed, or they may entail the erosion of previously established rights. Results also may be paradoxical or contradictory. The growth of rights for one social group may involve a contraction of rights among others. The rights of women to control their own bodies may conflict with the claim of citizenship rights for fetuses. The claims of natural and surrogate parents over transplanted embryos often clash. Animal rights claims do not accord with many Native people's demands for fishing and hunting rights. The aims of elderly citizens who wish to work past the standard retirement age conflict with those of younger workers in need of employment.

Rights struggles may be resisted, reversed and undermined. Because they frequently challenge existing arrangements and alliances of power and authority, rights movements are likely to be met by political resistance on behalf of dominant groups who seek to preserve the status quo. The resort to rights strategies may also oversimplify complex power relations and resolve social wrongs in an entirely individual manner. They may be appropriated by the more powerful and may not empower a weaker group. Perhaps, as Carol Smart (1989, 146) suggests, "rights claims are becoming less and less valuable . . . [even] counter-productive."

Yet it also should be borne in mind that rights struggles and movements, such as occurred around citizenship claims, have a universalizing logic and a contagious effect. They reduce particularistic and ascriptive bases to exclusivity. Moreover, as Turner (1986, 104) notes:

> Social movements provide models of change for subsequent groups in their struggle for rights and membership in society. . . . The struggle of protestors against the war in Vietnam provided a model for struggles for civil libertarians and in particular it galvanized American women and formed the basis for subsequent women's movements.

Rights struggles establish "flashpoints" for opposition. For example, the struggle for citizenship undercut the capacity of private capital to accumulate through profits, "since the expansion of social and political rights was translated into increased taxation, state regulation of the market and legislation to control the inheritance of property" (ibid., 1137). Similarly, rights struggles are typically employed as critiques of capitalism via the welfare society and welfare state. Rights movements often expand at the cost of hierarchical control over the polity, firm, and home. Once rights are won and institutionalized, they contribute an essential social valourization for political and legal change. Smart (1989, 143) also observes that rights have an appeal. They constitute a political language of considerable public access through which interests can be advanced and the state forced to listen. To launch a reform in terms of rights is a major step towards recognizing social wrongs, popularizing the claims of the struggle, and affording a measure of protection for the weak. Rights endow emergent alternative social movements with legitimacy and become an integral part of the continuing struggle of radical reform. Women, for example, fought to own property, to be recognized as legal persons, to be enfranchised and to obtain increased rights around abortion, divorce and custody. These rights are part and parcel of today's women's movement.

The social movement against corporate crime ought not to allow the profit squeeze to produce a civil liberties or rights squeeze. Rights struggles can radically alter the debate on corporate crime by moving the focus of reform away from a defensive position and towards "defining certain socially desired goals in terms of positive rights" (Sargent 1990, 110). For example, the right to a clean environment, the right to a safe workplace, and the right to a minimum wage are claims that increase the price capital must pay for legitimacy. As Snider (1987, 58) notes, class and rights discourses "create interstices within capitalism" whereby a new consensus "on the minimum level of misery" and on the "minimum standard for corporate behavior" may result. Hills (1987, 202) rightly observes:

> Until more citizens perceive that assaulting a woman's body with a dangerously designed birth control device is as serious as assaulting her in the streets; that concealing the level of cotton dust particles is as unconscionable a crime as mugging an old man in an alleyway; that manufacturing and keeping on the market a defective car known to explode and burn on rear-end impact is as morally repugnant as any conventional form of criminal manslaughter — only when such acts are defined as "real crimes" will further fundamental reform of the criminal justice system be possible.

Rights as the basis for regulatory intervention challenges the corporate sector's exclusive claim to resist state regulation as a matter of their "right." A new debate around the reasons for state intervention in the marketplace is created. Moral boundaries may be moved not in the name of a coercive public interest but on the strength of protecting individual or collective rights, backed up, of course, with the threat of civil or administrative sanctions. Moreover, as Sargent (1990, 111) observes, "appropriating rights discourse as the basis for regulatory intervention could turn out to be a powerful ideological weapon in favour of more effective enforcement." Framing the justification for regulation and control in terms of rights claims does not preclude the use of penal sanctions where a clear and persistent pattern of violation is established. The criminal culpability of corporations is still recognized, setting the stage for further extensions of corporate liability.

The increasing number of class and rights struggles and claims may also have a dialectical effect on the social and moral context that brought them about in the first place. They sharpen and underscore what constitutes lawful or unlawful corporate behaviour and, combined with censure and sanction, rights struggles strengthen emergent moral boundaries, which in turn create new pressures for holding corporations socially responsible and criminally liable. As Cullen, Maakestad and Cavender (1987, 335) observe of the struggle to redress the damage caused by the Ford Pinto automobile:

> Perhaps the most significant legacy of the past two decades is that people have come to think differently about corporations: about the potential for executives to pursue profits at any cost, about the harm that companies can inflict, about the social

responsibility that business should exercise and about what
constitutes a tolerable level of risk as corporate decisions affect
the welfare of workers, consumers, and entire communities.

Significantly, the key impetus behind these changes in moral param-
eters was the power of the social movement lined up against corporate
crime. As Kramer (1989, 155) notes:

> The Civil Rights movement, the new left, the consumer move-
> ment . . . the anti war movement, the environmental movement
> and the liberation movements of women and gays . . . laid bare
> the contradictions of the political economy and directed our
> attention to the crimes of the powerful. The moral crusaders and
> social activists who led these movements (some of whom were
> criminologists) have played a far greater role . . . against corpo-
> rate crime than have federal prosecutors.

Tudivier (1986) and Armstrong and Armstrong (1983), for example, note
that the establishment of women's health networks and women's labour
unions have been at the forefront of the fight against corporate dumping
of hazardous products and for health and safety in the workplace.
Without the development of these organizations, drugs and medical
devices such as the IUD would be marketed without resistance, and
corporate violence against women in the workplace would remain
unchecked.

Similarly, in the case of Union Carbide's destruction of the community of Bhopal in India, Pearce and Tombs (1989, 138) argue that any
genuine and lasting gains over corporate capital "will have to be *won* by
means of political struggle," and that effective engagement in the struggle
against corporate crime could bring the question of law and order in the
suites onto the popular agenda. They show that most industrial pollution, harm and death results from mismanagement of capital. Their
solutions to corporate crime are fivefold. First, communities, workers
and countries must mobilize and force corporations to adopt adequate
standard operating procedures and develop methods of effectively monitoring compliance with them. Second, workers must gain rights within
corporations. They should seek to participate in the monitoring of
internal compliance systems and force improvements upon management. "Right to know" arguments and legislation, along with appeals to
safer records and long-term general business efficiency, are particularly
useful levers with which to launch corporate reform. Third, real gains
have been won and should continue to be won in terms of the provision

of health and safety in the workplace. Corporations do have room to manoeuvre. Though accumulation is the clear priority, capital may be forced, cajoled or persuaded to accept the proposition that a safer and healthier workplace could also be an economically more efficient one. Corporate capital may even be convinced to accept a greater proportion of the economic cost of occupationally related reforms. As Pearce and Tombs (1990, 436) aptly put it, "health and safety provisions should not constitute 'added' costs for those engaged in economic activity. . . . The costs of such regulations are themselves costs of production." Fourth, political struggles must seek to democratize the coercively disciplinarian and authoritarian management regimes of capital. Finally, legal pressures will have to be placed on corporate capital. Corporations need to be watched and policed, and penalty ought to be heavy for those who violate regulations. The greater the stigma attached to capital as a class, the more likely it may pre-emptively try to regulate and discipline its own unruly conduct (ibid., 136-37).

Snider (1987, 1990, 1991), in her evaluations of reform processes in corporate crime, argues that we must deconstruct corporate crime and the political strategies of regulation. Corporate crime is not a single homogenous entity. For example, occupational health and safety struggles, antitrust and monopoly strategies, insider trading and stock market fraud regulations and laws against environmental pollution have evinced distinct political economies of control, some clearly more successful than others. Real victories have been won in the areas of safety, health and working conditions. These have partly resulted from technological innovations but have primarily come about because unions, workers and their allies have fought hard and long to remove the risks and dangers and change the morality of the workplace. Corporations have been forced by public outrage or union agitation to accept that high accident rates were not profitable and to finance the costs of collective compensation programs (Snider, 1987, 1991).

Similarly, insider trading and stock market frauds are relatively well regulated and policed when compared to other forms of corporate crime. Both capital and the state have been more or less willing partners in proactively monitoring and censoring many types of misconduct in the marketplace. In crimes of capital against capital, the political will appears to exist to safeguard the circuits and rules by which investment capital flows. There are thus powerful *internal* pressures for regulation, although it must be cautioned that there are also forces out to "make a killing" at any cost, as the failure of more than 300 U.S. savings and loans companies so dramatically illustrates. Nevertheless, economic losses to capital as a class make it more likely that collective goals will temper excessive individual corporate greed because capital as a whole and the state will suffer from such imprecations. As Snider (1991, 209-10) notes, the cost of the Drexel Burnham bailout is estimated "at $325 billion at minimum, $500 billion more realistically, and $1.4 trillion according to yet another estimate. . . . This massive market fraud is expected to cost every household in the USA a minimum of $5,000." Clearly there are incentives to regulate in this area of corporate crime. Reform strategies are more likely to be successful if they make fraud and racketeering activities visible and highlight the relationship of these types of corporate crime to structural factors and values central to the organization and reproduction of legal capital (Snider, 1990).

Less progress has been made by rights movements towards protecting the environment and controlling antitrust/monopoly illegalities. In the case of the latter, the entrenched interests of transnational corporations have dominated. Pro-regulatory groups have been few and their pressure minimal. Enforcement has been generally weak and ineffective. Indeed Coleman (1989), Hopkins (1979) and Goff and Reasons (1978) have shown that antimonopoly laws are a record of repeated failure. Clearly the issues around antitrust laws are complex and often "there is no clear beneficiary — except perhaps consumers, a weak pressure group at best, and one with little moral clout. It is not obvious that the 'right' to buy a product at a cheap price should automatically take precedence over the right of workers to jobs, or the right of the public to a clean environment" (Snider 1991, 224). The state is an uncertain ally in this particular struggle — it is ambivalent at best and co-opted at worst. The social movement against corporate crime has a major struggle on its hands. New, bold and imaginative strategies will have to publicize the harms of transnationals (inefficiency, dependency, concentration of power, lack of accountability, etc.) and mobilize the state and the public to challenge the claims of corporate capital not to have to compete fairly in the marketplace.

Environmental protection may represent a struggle with greater promise than performance would indicate thus far. Though control over corporate polluters has been weak and ineffective, public support remains strong for regulatory action. According to Snider (1991, 229), reforms to work towards include those that create new rights to environmental integrity and those that make damage and degradation unprofitable. As in the health and safety field, this will entail ideological struggle: identifying victims, redefining the levels of risk and despoilation acceptable to the environment and "determining new rights and responsibilities for corporations, unions, states, and communities as they relate to the environment." Again reforms will occur only when they are forced upon a reluctant corporate class.

In raising such proposals, these authors and others already mentioned direct our attention to one important fact: there will be no effective remedies to corporate crime unless there is a vigilant social movement willing and prepared to challenge the power and privilege of corporate capital. This is no easy task, for "those who have the interest in fundamental change have not the power, while those who have the power have not the interest" (Parenti 1980, 312). However, we must guard against pessimism. As we have seen, the might of corporate capital is considerable and the development of rights struggles will be bought at a social cost: more bureaucracy, more surveillance, and more public regulation of social life. As Smart (1989, 162) puts it, "More rights come at the cost of the potential for greater surveillance and greater conformity and the claim for new rights brings about the possibility of new forms of regulation." Perhaps the fatalistic mood that characterizes the sociology of bureaucracy, politics and industrialization is correct. Do good intentions inevitably have bad consequences, as many economists and sociologists seem to think? If so, the sad conclusion may be that the attack on corporate crime will abate. Public condemnation may wane and moral indignation may decline. The legitimacy gap affecting corporate credibility may close. Moral boundaries may return to those of past banalities, and criminal justice politics may lose its new-found resolve to prosecute the powerful. The will to control corporations may atrophy in the withering light of corporate might. This would be a depressing end to our story and a serious indictment of the principles of social justice. Box (1983, 78-79) sees the issue clearly:

> Can it be justified to send to prisons people too poor to pay fines
> . . . when their crime is trivial in the extreme in comparison with
> corporate crimes. . . . Can it be right to send people to prison
> because they have been found guilty of drunkenness, vagrancy,
> . . . prostitution and drug offences . . . theft, handling stolen
> property, fraud, and forgery, when the amounts of value in-
> volved are nothing in comparison with the millions stolen by
> offending corporations on whom our criminal justice system has
> given up?

Is there another conclusion? Can those who have the power be made to have an interest in altering their dangerous and predatory behaviour? Certainly, as this book has demonstrated, many enterprising ideas have emerged for the control of corporate crime and for the reorganization of large corporations to meet public needs. A popular will is now growing to limit the atrocity of corporate carnage. The consensus seems to be that a more socialized means of production is necessary if we are to keep our lives, limbs and property safe from transnational corporate harm and theft. Like other social rights struggles, the process is going to be radical, protracted and socially disruptive. Like other struggles, there will be victories and reversals. The road to radical reform has many twists and turns. But precisely because corporate capitalism is inherently violent, harmful, exploitative and homicidal, it creates a context in which progressive forces will likely continue to develop. In this sense, monopoly capitalism creates the conditions for its own transformation and transcendence, in that the conditions for social justice grow out of the struggle for genuine rights in and against capitalism. Along the way, capitalism may be transformed. The state, popular working class institutions, trade unions, women's organizations, etc., have changed, at least partly, the features of capitalism. Ironically, bad intentions have had unintended beneficial consequences. As Turner (1986, 142) observes:

> The anarchy of the marketplace creates the conditions for the development of the state as that institution which guarantees social contracts and provides an administration within which profits can be realized, but the state also becomes an institution necessary for the protection and development of social rights. Capitalism is transformed by a set of institutions which were designed to maintain and protect its continuity.

So we need not be cynical or despairing. But the social movement against corporate crime is going to have to increase its profile and continue to flex its muscles. Workers, consumers, environmentalists and victims of corporate crime will have to continue to demand and redemand their rights. Corporations will have to be forced to change. Rarely will they do so of their own accord. Symbolic victories, while important, need to be extended into substantive policy and political changes.

The price of social justice will have to be a curb on private profits, and the social management of corporations for the public good. This entails a radical restructuring: nationalizing the worst corporate offenders, establishing government ownership of key sectors of the economy, democratizing the workplace and government institutions and planning, legislating a progressive tax system and limiting the transfer of wealth and privilege via inheritance and tax-exempt foundations, implementing a program of progressive income redistribution, expanding a program of social and community construction, developing a national ecological plan compatible with living in an industrial world and reorganizing investment and corporate structures so public interests are given as much consideration as those of corporate capital.

I hope, in conclusion, that this book has enlarged your vision of what constitutes criminal violence and helped you to see clearly the connections between the drive for capital accumulation, the callous culture of corporate bureaucracy, the negligent legal system, the hesitant state, and the production and reproduction of corporate crime. I have argued that the scope and seriousness of corporate crime is enormous, far exceeding that of conventional crime. As such it is a major element of "the crime problem." This is not to underplay the significance of predatory street crime, which represents a grave social problem and needs to be theorized and fought against (Lea and Young 1984; Kinsey et al. 1986; Currie 1985). Yet, arguably, crimes of capital are even more dangerous and disquieting. Necessarily, the political priorities of critical criminology need to be re-evaluated to include law and order in the suites.

I also hope this study has effectively communicated that something can be done about corporate crime, despite the difficulties in detecting, monitoring and controlling it effectively and despite the high costs of social control itself to society. I suspect what we know about many of these issues is incomplete and insufficient. But we do have enough specialized knowledge of the corporate criminalization process, the social control of corporate organizations and the causes and rationalizations that allow the perpetuation of corporate crime to be of use to those working for structural change. I hope this book may serve as an example of "criminological interventionism," that its ideas may be of use to activists and reformers who seek to prevent and bring under control the suffering, financial loss and death caused by corporate crime and violence. If theory is the process whereby people become aware of the conditions of their life and formulate ideas based on their needs and aspirations for social change, then I believe these ideas will gain force by being fused with the social movement against corporate crime.

References

Albanese, J.
1984   "Love Canal Six Years Later: The Legal Legacy."
            Federal Probation 48 (June).

Anderson, D.
1981   "The Curse of the Corporate Vampires." *MacLeans* 94
            (March): 26-30.

Armstrong, P., and H. Armstrong
1983   *A Working Majority: What Women Do For Pay.* Ottawa:
            Canadian Advisory Council on the Status of Women.

Auf der Maur, N.
1976   *The Billion Dollar Game.* Toronto: James Lorimer.

Ball, H.V., and L.W. Friedman
1968   "The Use of Criminal Sanctions in the Enforcement of
            Economic Legislation: A Sociological View." In G. Geis (ed.),
            *White Collar Criminal: The Offender in Business and the Pro-
            fessions.* New York: Atherton Press.

Baran, P.A., and P.M. Sweezy
1966   *Monopoly Capital.* New York: Monthly Review Press.

Bardach, E., and R.A. Kagan
1982   *Going By the Book: The Problem of Regulatory Unreasonableness.*
            Philadelphia: Temple University Press.

Barnett, H.
1981   "Corporate Capitalism, Corporate Crime." *Crime and
            Delinquency* 27.

Benjamin, J.
1989   *The Bonds of Love. Psychoanalysis, Feminism and the Problem of
            Domination.* New York: Pantheon Books

Bequai, A.
1978   *White Collar Crime: A 20th Century Crisis.* Toronto: Lexington
            Books.

Bliss, M.
1974   *A Living Profit: Studies in the Social History of Canadian
            Business, 1883-1911.* Toronto: McClelland and Stewart.

Blum, R. H.
1972   *Deceivers and Deceived.* Springfield, Ill: Charles Thomas.

Bowles, S., and R. Edwards
1985   *Understanding Capitalism.* New York: Harper and
            Row.

Bowles, S., D.M. Gordon, and T.E. Weisskopf
1985   *Beyond the Wasteland: A Democratic Alternative to
            Economic Decline.* Garden City, N.Y.: Doubleday/
            Anchor.

Box, S.
1983   *Power Crime and Mystification.* London: Tavistock
            Books.

Braithwaite, J.
1978   "An Exploratory Study of Used Car Fraud." In P.
            Wilson and J. Braithwaite (eds.), *Two Faces of Deviance.* St.
            Lucia: University of Queensland Press.

Braithwaite, J.
1979a   "Corporate Crime: Regulating Corporate Behavior Through
            Criminal Sanctions." *Harvard Law Review* 92, no. 6: 1227-75.

Braithwaite, J.
1979b   "Transnational Corporations and Corruption: Towards
            Some International Solutions." *International Journal of the
            Sociology of Law* 7: 125-42.

Braithwaite, J.
1982   "Enforced Self-Regulation: A New Strategy for Corporate
            Crime Control." *Michigan Law Review* 80, no. 7: 1466-1507.

Braithwaite, J., and G. Geis
1982   "On Theory and Action for Corporate Crime Control."
            Crime and Delinquency 28 (April).

Braithwaite, J., and B. Fisse
1983   "Asbestos and Health: A Case of Informal Control."
            Australian-New Zealand Journal of Criminology 16: 67-80.

Braithwaite, J.
1984   *Corporate Crime in the Pharmaceutical Industry.* London:
            Routledge and Kegan Paul.

Braithwaite, J., and B. Fisse
1985   "Varieties of Responsibility and Organizational Crime." *Law
            and Policy* 7: 315-43.

Braithwaite, J.
1989   *Crime, Shame and Reintegration.* New York: Cambridge
            University Press.

Braithwaite, J.
1991   "Poverty, Power, White Collar Crime and the Paradoxes of Criminological Theory." *Australian and New Zealand Journal of Criminology* 24: 40-58.

Braul, W., J. Russel, and W.J. Andrews
1989   *Toxic Real Estate in British Columbia: Identification of Issues.* Vancouver: West Coast Environmental Law Research Foundation.

Brickey, S., and E. Comack
1987   "The Role of Law in Social Transformation: Is a Jurisprudence of Insurgency Possible." *Canadian Journal of Law and Society* 2.

Brittan, A.
1989   *Masculinity and Power.* Oxford: Basil Blackwell.

Brodeur, P.
1985   *Outrageous Misconduct: The Asbestos Industry on Trial.* New York: Pantheon.

Brenner, S.S., and E.A. Molander
1977   "Is the Ethics of Business Changing?" *Harvard Business Review* (January-February): 66-76.

Brown, M.
1979   *Laying Waste: The Poisoning of America by Toxic Chemicals.* New York: Pantheon.

Cahan, V., and D. Moskowitz
1985   "A Murder Verdict Jolts Business." *Business Week,* July 1.

Canada.
1981   *The State of Competition in the Canadian Petroleum Industry.* Ottawa: Department of Consumer and Corporate Affairs.

Canada, and Newfoundland and Labrador.
1984   *Royal Commission on the Ocean Ranger Marine Disaster, Report One: The Loss of the Semisubmersible Drill Rig Ocean Ranger and its Crew.* Ottawa: Minister of Supply and Services.

Caputo, T.
1989   "Political Economy, Law and Environmental Protection." In T. Caputo, M. Kennedy, C.E. Reason, and A. Brannigan (eds.), Law and Society: A Critical Perspective. Toronto: Harcourt Brace Jovanovich.

Carey, J.T.
1978   Introduction to Criminology. Engelwood Cliffs, N.J.: Prentice-Hall.

Carey, J.T.
    1987   "Benton Harlow: Distributor of Unsafe Drugs." In S. Hills
                    (ed.), Corporate Violence: Injury and Death for Profit.
                    Totowa, N.J.: Rowman and Littlefield.

Carson, W.G.
    1970   "White Collar Crime and the Enforcement of Factory
                    Legislation." British Journal of Criminology 10: 383-98.

Carson, W.G.
    1980a   "The Institutionalisation of Ambiguity: Early British Factory
                    Acts." In G. Geis and E. Stotland (eds.), White Collar Crime:
                    Theory and Research. Beverly Hills, Calif.: Sage.

Carson, W.G.
    1980b   "The Other Price of Britain's Oil: Regulating Safety on
                    Offshore Oil Relations in the British Sector of the North
                    Sea." Contemporary Crises 4, no. 3: 252-66.

Carson, W.G.
    1982   The Other Price of Britain's Oil. New Brunswick, N.J.:
                    Rutgers University Press.

Casey, J.
    1985   Corporate Crime and the State: Canada in the 1980's." In T.
                    Fleming (ed.), The New Criminologies in Canada. Toronto:
                    Oxford University Press.

Castrilli, J.
    1982   "Control of Toxic Chemicals in Canada: An Analysis of Law
                    and Policy." Osgoode Hall Law Journal no. 2 (June): 322-
                    401.

Cavanagh, J., and F. Clairmonte
    1983   "From Corporations to Conglomerates." Multinational
                    Monitor 4 (January): 16-20.

Chenier, N. M.
    1982   Reproductive Hazards at Work: Men, Women and the
                    Fertility Gamble. Ottawa: Canadian Advisory Council on
                    the Status of Women.

Cheslatta Band
    1991a   "Individual Statements Re: Before and After Surrender."
                    Burns Lake, B.C., mimeograph.

Cheslatta Band
    1991b   "The Story of the Surrender of the Cheslatta Reserves."
                    Burns Lake, B.C., mimeograph.

Chibnall, S., and P. Saunders
1977   "Worlds Apart: Notes on the Social Relativity of
            Corruption." British Journal of Sociology 28: 138-54.

Churchill, W.
1991   "Genocide in Arizona? The Navajo-Hopi Land Dispute in
            Perspective." In Ward Churchill (ed.), Critical Issues in
            Native North America vol. II. Copenhagen: IWGIA
            document no. 68: 104-46.

Churchill, W., and W. LaDuke
1991   "Native America: The Political Economy of Radioactive
            Colonialism." In Ward Churchill (ed.), Critical Issues in
            Native North America vol. II. Copenhagen: IWGIA
            document no. 68: 25-67.

Claybrook, J.
1984   *Retreat from Safety: Reagan's Attack on America's Safety.*
            New York: Pantheon Books.

Clement, W.
1975   The Canadian Corporate Elite. Toronto: McClelland and
            Stewart.

Clement, W.
1977   Continental Corporate Power: Economic Linkages Between
            Canada and the United States. Toronto: McClelland and
            Stewart.

Clinard, M. B.
1978   Cities with Little Crime: The Case of Switzerland. New
            York: Cambridge University Press.

Clinard, M. B.
1979   Illegal Corporate Behaviour. Washington, D.C.: National
            Institute of Law Enforcement and Criminal Justice.

Clinard, M.B., P.C. Yeager, J.M. Brissette, D. Petrashek and E. Harries
1979   Illegal Corporate Behavior. Washington, D.C.: U.S.
            Government Printing Office.

Clinard, M. B., and P.C. Yeager eds.
1980   Corporate Crime. New York: The Free Press.

Clinard, M. B.
1983   Corporate Ethics and Crime: the Role of Middle
            Management. Beverly Hills, Calif.: Sage.

Cockburn, C.
1985   Machinery of Dominance: Women, Men and Technical
            Know-How. London: Pluto Press.

Coffee, J.C.
1980   "Corporate Crime and Punishment: A Non-Chicago View of the Economics of Criminal Sanctions." American Criminal Law Review 17: 419-76.

Coffee, J. C.
1981   "'No Soul to Damn, No Body to Kick': An Unscandalized Inquiry into the Problems of Corporate Punishment." Michigan Law Review (January): 386-459.

Cohen, L.E., and R. Machalek
1988   "A General Theory of Expropriative Crime: An Evolutionary Ecological Approach." American Journal of Sociology 94: 465-501.

Coleman, J.W.
1989   The Criminal Elite: the Sociology of White Collar Crime. New York: St. Martin's Press.

Collinson, D.L., and M. Collinson
1989   "Sexuality in the Workplace: The Domination of Men's Sexuality." In J. Hearn, D.L. Sheppard, P. Tancred-Sheriff and G. Burrel (eds.), *The Sexuality of Organization*. London: Sage.

Conklin, J.E.
1977   Illegal but Not Criminal: Business Crime in America. Englewood Cliffs, N.J.: Prentice-Hall.

Cook, D.
1989   "Fiddling Tax and Benefits: Inculpating the Poor, Exculpating the Rich." In P. Carlen and D. Cook (eds., Paying for Crime. Milton Keynes: Open University Press.

Cook, F.J.
1966   The Corrupted Land: The *Social Morality of Modern America*. New York: MacMillan.

Cranston, R.
1982   "Regulation and DeRegulation: General Issues." University of New South Wales Law Journal 5: 1-29.

Cressey, D.R.
1953   Other People's Money: A Study in the Social Psychology of Embezzlement. Belmont, Calif.: Wadsworth.

Cressey, D.R.
1976   "Restraints of Trade, Recidivism, and Delinquent Neighbourhoods." In James Short (ed.), Delinquency, Crime and Society. Chicago: University of Chicago Press.

Croft, R.
1975   Swindle: A Decade of Canadian Stock Frauds. Toronto:
               Gage.

Cullen, F.T., B.G. Link, and C.W. Polanzi
1982   "The Seriousness of Crime Revisited: Have Attitudes
               Towards White Collar Crime Changed?" Criminology 20:
               83-102.

Cullen, F.T., G. Clark, R. Mathers and J. Cullen
1983   "Public Support for Punishing White Collar Crime: Blaming
               the Victim Revisited." Journal of Criminal Justice 11: 481-93.

Cullen, F.T., and P.J. Dubeck
1985   "The Myth of Corporate Immunity to Deterrence: Ideology
               and the Creation of the Invincible Criminal." Federal
               Probation 49 (September): 3-9.

Cullen, F.T., W. Maakestad and G. Cavender
1987   Corporate Crime Under Attack: The Ford Pinto Case and
               Beyond. Cincinnati: Anderson.

Currie, E.
1985   Confronting Crime: An American Challenge. New York:
               Pantheon.

DeKeseredy, W., and R. Hinch
1991   Woman Abuse: Sociological Perspectives. Toronto:
               Thompson.

Denzin, N.
1977   "Notes on the Criminogenic Hypothesis: A Case Study of
               the American Liquor Industry." American Sociological
               Review .42: no. 6: 905-20.

Dershowitz, A.
1968   "Increasing Community Control Over Corporate Crime: A
               Problem in the Law of Sanctions." In G. Geis (ed.), White
               Collar Criminal: The Offender in Business and the
               Professions. New York: Atherton Press.

Dewey, M.
1982   "Hazardous Waste Time Bomb Still Ticking." Globe and
               Mail, February 28: B1.

Director of Investigations and Research
1965   Combines Investigation Act Report. Ottawa: Queens Printer.

Director of Investigations and Research
1975   Combines Investigation Act Report. Ottawa: Information
               Canada.

DiTomaso, N.
  1989   "Sexuality in the Workplace: Discrimination and
                Harrassment." In J. Hearn, D.L. Sheppard, P. Tancred-
                Sheriff and G. Burrel (eds.), *The Sexuality of Organization.*
                London: Sage.

Dowie, M.
  1977   "How Ford Put Two Million Firetraps on Wheels." Business
                and Society Review (fall): 41.

Dowie, M.
  1979   "Pinto Madness." In Jerome H. Skolnick and Elliott Currie
                (eds.), Crisis in American Institutions, 4th edition, Boston:
                Little Brown.

Dowie, M.
  1987a   "The Dumping of Hazardous Products on Foreign
                Markets." In Stuart Hills (ed.), Corporate Violence, Injury
                and Death for Profit. Tatowa, N.J.: Rowman and Littlefield.

Dowie, M.
  1987b   "Pinto Madness." In Stuart Hills (ed.), Corporate Violence,
                Injury and Death for Profit Tatowa, N.J.: Rowman and
                Littlefield.

Dworkin, R.
  1977   Taking Rights Seriously. London: Duckworth.

Ellis, D.
  1986   The Wrong Stuff. Toronto: Collier McMillan.

Epstein, S.
  1979   The Politics of Cancer. New York: Anchor Books.

Erikson, K.
  1976   Everything In Its Path: Destruction of Community in the
                Buffalo Creek Flood. New York: Simon and Schuster.

Erikson, K.
  1985   "Foreword." In Anastasia Shkilnyk, A Poison Stronger Than
                Love. New Haven: Yale University Press.

Ermann, M. D. and R. J. Lundman
  1978a   "Deviant Acts by Complex Organizations: Deviance and
                Social Control at the Organizational Level of Analysis." In
                S.L. Messinger and E. Bittner (eds.), Criminology Review
                Yea*rbook*. Beverly Hills, Calif.: Sage.

Ermann, M.D. and R.J. Lundman, eds.
  1978b   Corporate and Governmental Deviance: Problems of
                Organizational Behavior in Contemporary Society. New
                York: Oxford University Press.

Ermann, M.D. and Lundman, R.J.
1982   Corporate Deviance. New York: Holt, Rinehart & Winston.

Everest, L.
1986   Behind the Poison Cloud: Union Carbide's Bhopal Massacre.
              New York: Banner Press.

Farberman, H.A
1975   "A Criminogenic Market Structure: The Automobile
              Industry." Sociological Quarterly 16 (autumn): 438-57.

Fattah, E.A.
1976   Deterrence: A Review of the Literature. Ottawa: Supply and
              Services.

Faulkner, P.
1987   "Exposing Risks of Nuclear Disaster: Confessions of a
              Whistle Blower." In S. Hills (ed.), Corporate Violence: Injury
              and Death for Profits. Totowa, N.J.: Rowman and Littlefield.

Feinberg, J.
1970   "The Expressive Function of Punishment." In J. Feinberg
              (ed.), Doing and Deserving. Princeton: Princeton University
              Press.

Fellmeth, R.
1973   "The Regulatory-Industrial Complex"." In R. Nader (ed.),
              The Common and Corporate Accountability. New York:
              Harcourt Brace Jovanovich.

Ferguson, K.
1984   The Feminist Case Against Bureaucracy. Philadelphia:
              Temple University Press.

Finney, H.C., and H.R. Lessieur
1982   "A Contingency Theory of Organizational Crime." In S.B.
              Bacharach (ed.), Research in the Sociology of Organizations.
              Greenwich, Conn.: JAI Press.

Fisse, B., and J. Braithwaite
1983   The Impact of Publicity on Corporate Offenders. Albany:
              State University of New York.

Ford, A.R.
1986   "Hormones: Getting out of Hands." In K. McDonnell (ed.),
              Adverse Effects: Women and the Pharmaceutical Industry.
              Toronto: Women's Press.

Francis, D.
1986   Controlling Interest: Who Owns Canada? Toronto:
              Macmillan.

Francis, D.
    1988   Contrepreneurs. Toronto: Macmillan

Frank, N.
    1985   Crimes Against Health and Safety. New York: Harrow and
                  Heston.

Galanter, M.
    1974   "Why the Haves Come Out Ahead." Law and Society
                  Review 9: 95-160.

Geis, G.
    1973   "Deterring Corporate Crime." In Ralph Nader and Mark J.
                  Green (eds.), Corporate Power in America. New York:
                  Grossman.

Geis, G.
    1978   "White Collar Crime: The Heavy Electrical Equipment
                  Antitrust Case of 1961." In David Ermann and Richard
                  Lundman (eds.), Corporate and Government Deviance.
                  New York: Oxford University Press.

Geis, G.
    1984   "Upper World Crime." In Current Perspectives on Criminal
                  Behaviour: Original Essays in Criminology. New York:
                  Knopf.

Giddens, A.
    1981   A Contemporary Critique of Historical Materialism.
                  London: Macmillan.
Gill, I.
    1991   "Surrender." The Georgia Straight, July 19-26.

Gilligan, C.
    1982   *In A Different Voice.* London: Harvard University Press.

Glassbeek, H.J., and S. Rowland
    1979   "Are Injuring and Killing at Work Crimes?" Osgoode Hall
                  Law Journal 17.

Glassbeek, H.J.
    1989   "Why Corporate Deviance is Not Treated as a Crime." In T.
                  Caputo, M. Kennedy, C. Reasons and A. Brannigan (eds.),
                  Law and *Society: A Critical Perspective.* Toronto: Harcourt
                  Brace Jovanovich.

Globe and Mail
    1991   "The Godfather of Hull." June 22.

Globe and Mail
    1991   "Bankrupt firm's assets must go to cleanup." July 12.

Globe and Mail
1991   "Top Tory Politicians, Law Enforcers Charged in Ottawa."
               July 18.

Globe and Mail
1991   "Tory Accused Express Surprise." July 19.

Globe and Mail
1991   "Crusader may rain on P.M.'s Sept 16 parade." July 20.

Globe and Mail
1991   "Maxwell accused of share-support schemes." December 9.

Globe and Mail
1991   "Maxwell troubles deepen." December 10.

Goff, C.H., and C.E. Reasons
1978   Corporate Crime in Canada: A Critical Analysis of Anti-
                combines Legislation. Englewood Cliffs, N.J.: Prentice-Hall.

Goff, C.H. and C.E. Reasons
1986   "Organizational Crimes Against Employees, Consumers,
                and the Public." In Brian MacLean (ed.), The Political
                Economy of Crime. Scarborough: Prentice Hall.

Goff, C.H., and N. Mason-Clark
1989   "The Seriousness of Crime in Fredericton, New Brunswick:
                Perceptions Toward White-Collar Crime." Canadian Journal
                of Criminology 31 (1): 19-34.

Goffman, E.
1964   Stigma: Notes on the Management of Spoiled Identity.
                Englewood Cliffs, N.J.: Prentice-Hall.

Gordon, R., and I. Coneybeer
1991   "Corporate Crime." In Margaret Jackson and Curt Griffiths
                (eds.), Canadian Criminology: Perspectives on Crime and
                Criminality. Toronto: Harcourt Brace Jovanovich.

Gough, I.
1979   The Political Economy of the Welfare State. London:
                MacMillan.

Graham, J.M., and V.H. Kramer
1976   Appointments to the Regulatory Agencies: The Federal
                Communications Commission and the Federal Trade
                Commission. Washington: U.S. Government Printing Office.

Green, M., and J. Berry
1985   The Challenge of Hidden Profits. New York: Morrow.

Gross, E.
    1978a   "Organizational Crime: A Theoretical Perspective." In
                 Norman Denzin (ed.), Studies in Symbolic Interactionism.
                 Greenwick: I.A.I. Press.
Gross, E.
    1978b   "Organizations as Criminal Actors." In Paul Wilson and
                 John Braithwaite (eds.), Two Faces of Deviance: Crimes of
                 the Powerless and the Powerful. St. Lucia: University of
                 Queensland.

Gunningham, N.
    1974   Pollution, Social Interest and the Law. London: Martin
                 Robertson.

Gutek, B.
    1989   "Sexuality in the Workplace: Key Issues in Social Research
                 and Organizational Practice." In J. Hearn, D.L. Sheppard, P.
                 Tancred-Sheriff and G. Burrel (eds.), *The Sexuality of
                 Organization*. London: Sage.

Hadden, T.
    1983   "Fraud in the City: The Role of the Criminal Law." *Criminal
                 Law Review* (August).

Hagan, J., and P. Parker
    1985   "White Collar Crime and Punishment: The Class Structure
                 and the Legal Sanctioning of Securities Violations."
                 American Sociological Review 50 (June): 302-16.

Hagan, J.
    1987   "White Collar and Corporate Crime." In Rick Linden (ed.),
                 Criminology: A Canadian Perspective. Toronto: Holt,
                 Rinehart and Winston.

Harding, J.
    1986   "Mood-modifiers and Elderly Women in Canada: The
                 Medicalization of Poverty." In K. McDonnell (ed.), Adverse
                 Effects: Women and the Pharmaceutical Industry. Toronto:
                 Women's Press.

Harding, J.
    1989   "Indigenous Rights and Uranium Mining in Northern
                 Saskatchewan." In Ward Churchill (ed.), Critical Issues in
                 Native North America, vol I. Copenhagen: IWGIA
                 document no. 67: 116-36.

Harvard Law Review
    1979   "Developments in the Law. Corporate Crime: Regulating
                 Corporate Behaviour Through Criminal Sanctions." Vol.92:
                 1229-1375.

Heilbroner, R.L.
1985   The Nature and Logic of Capitalism. New York: W.W.
                   Norton and Co.

Henry, F.
1986   "Crime: A Profitable Approach." In Brian MacLean (ed.),
                   The Political Economy of Crime. Scarborough: Prentice Hall.

Herring, E.P.
1936   Federal Commissioners: A Study of Their Careers and
                   Qualifications. Cambridge, Mass: Harvard University Press.

Hills, S.
1987   "Corporate Violence and the Banality of Evil." In Stuart
                   Hills (ed.), Corporte Violence, Injury and Death for Profit.
                   Tatowa, N.J.: Rowman and Littlefield.

Hopkins, A.
1978   Crime, Law, and Business: the Sociological Sources of
                   Australian Monopoly Law. Canberra: Australian Institute of
                   Criminology.

Hopkins, A.
1979   "The Anatomy of Corporate Crime." In Paul R. Wilson and
                   John Braithwaite (eds.), Two Faces of Deviance. St. Lucia:
                   Queensland Press.

Hopkins, A.
1980   "Controlling Corporate Deviance." Criminology 18: 198-214.

House, J.D.
1986   "Working Offshore: the other price of Newfoundland's oil."
                   In K.L.P. Lundy and B. Warme (eds.), Work in the Canadian
                   Context. Toronto: Butterworths.

Johnson, J.M., and J.D. Douglas, eds.
1978   Crime at the Top: Deviance in Business and the Professions.
                   Philadelphia: Lippincott.

Jones, P.T.
1985   "Sanctions, Incentives, and Corporate Behavior." California
                   Management Review 27 (spring).

Kadish, S.H.
1963   "Some Observations on the Use of Criminal Sanctions in
                   Enforcing Economic Regulations." University of Chicago
                   Law Review 30 (spring): 423-49.

Kagan, R. and J.T. Scholz
1983   "The Criminology of the Corporation and Regulatory
                   Enforcement Strategies." In K. Hawkins and J. Thomas
                   (eds.), Enforcing Regulation. Boston: Kluwer-Nijhoff.

Katz, J.
    1980   "The Social Movement Against White-Collar Crime." In E.
                  Bittner and S. L. Messinger (eds.), Criminology Review
                  Yearbook, vol. 2. Beverly Hills, Calif.: Gage.

Katz, J.
    1988   Seductions of Crime: Moral and Sensual Attractions of
                  Doing Evil. New York: Basic Books.

Keller, E.F.
    1985   Reflections on Gender and Science. New Haven: Yale
                  University Press.

Kesner, I., B. Victor and B. Lamont
    1986   "Board Composition and the Commission of Illegal Acts:
                  An Investigation of Fortune 500 Companies." Academy of
                  Management Journal 29 (December).

King, D.K.
    1985   "The Regulatory Use of the Criminal Sanction in Controlling
                  Corporate Crime." Paper presented at American Society of
                  Criminology meeting, San Diego, California, November.

Kinsey, J., J. Lea and J. Young
    1986   Losing the Fight Against Crime. Oxford: Basil Blackwell.

Kramer, R.C.
    1982   "Corporate Crime: An Organizational Perspective." In Peter
                  Wickman and Timothy Dailey (eds.), White Collar and
                  Economic Crime. Lexington: D.C. Heath.

Kramer, R.C.
    1989   "Criminologists and the Social Movement Against
                  Corporate Crime." Social Justice 16, no. 2: 146-64.

LaDuke, W.
    1990   "James Bay: A Northern Sacrifice Area." Z Magazine 3, no. 6
                  (June).

Lambert, R.
    1973   Sir John Simon 1816-1904, and English Social
                  Administration. London: Fitzgibbon and Kee.

Lane, R.E.
    1977   "Why Businessmen Violate the Law." In G. Geis and R.F.
                  Meier (eds.), *White Collar Crime*. New York: The Free Press.

Larsen, E.N.
    1981   "Lobbying the Canadian Way: An Analysis of Corporate
                  Crime in Canada." Canadian Criminology Forum 4: 23-29.

Law Reform Commission of Canada
    1986   "Workplace Pollution." Working paper no. 53. Ottawa: Law
                  Reform Commission of Canada.

Lea, J., and J. Young
1984   What is to be done about law and order? Harmondsworth:
            Penguin Books.

Leonard, W.,and M. Weber
1970   "Automakers and Dealers: A Study of Criminogenic Market
            Forces." Law and Society Review 4 (February): 406-14.

Levi, M.
1981   The Phantom Capitalists: The Organization and Control of
            Long-term Fraud. London: Heinemann.

Levi, M.
1984   "Giving Creditors the Business: the Criminal Law in
            Inaction." In International Journal of the Sociology of Law
            12, no. 3: 321-33.

Levi, M.
1989   "Fradulent Justice? Sentencing the Business Criminal." In P.
            Carlen and D. Cook (eds.), Paying for Crime. Milton Keynes:
            Open University Press.

Lloyd, G.
1984   The Man of Reason: Male and Female in Western
            Philosophy. London: Methuen.

Long, S.
1979   "The Internal Revenue Service: Examining the Exercise of
            Discretion." Paper presented at Law and Society Association
            annual meeting, May.

Lowe, R.
1977   "Why Businessmen Violate the Law." In G. Geis and R.F.
            Mercer (eds.), White Collar Crime. New York: The Free
            Press.

Lukes, S.
1987   Marxism and Morality. Oxford: Oxford University Press.

Luthans, F., and R.M. Hodgetts, eds.
1976   Social Issues in Business: A Text with Current Readings and
            Cases. New York: Macmillan.

Lynxwiller, J., N. Shover and D. Clelland
1983   "The Organization of Inspection Discretion in a Regulatory
            Bureaucracy." Social Problems 30 (April): 425-36.

Madden, C.
1977   "Forces Which Influence Ethical Behavior." In C. Madden
            (ed.), The Ethics of Corporate Conduct. Englewood Cliffs,
            N.J.: Prentice-Hall.

Marchak, P.M.
1979   In Whose Interest, An Essay on Multinational Corporations
            in a Canadian Context. Toronto: McClelland and Stewart.

Marchak, P.M.
    1988   Ideological Perspectives on Canada. Toronto: McGraw, Hill,
                    Ryerson.

Margolis, D.R.
    1979   The Managers: Corporate Life in America. New York:
                    Morrow.

Marx, K.
    1973   Capital. Volume 1. New York: International Publishers.

Matza, D.
    1969   Becoming Deviant. Englewood Cliffs, N.J.: Prentice-Hall.

McBarnett, H.C.
    1982   "The Production of Corporate Crime in Corporate
                    Capitalism." In Peter Wickman and Timothy Dailey (eds.),
                    White Collar and Economic Crime. Toronto: Lexington
                    Books.

McCormick, A.E.
    1977   "Rule Enforcement and Moral Indignation: Some
                    Observations on the Effects of Criminal Antitrust
                    Convictions Upon Societal Reaction Processes." Social
                    Problems 25 (October): 30-39.

McCormick, A.E.
    1979   Dominant Class Interests and the Emergence of Anti-Trust
                    Legislation." Contemporary Crises 3: 399-417.

McDermott, M.F.
    1982   "Occupational Disqualification of Corporate Executives: An
                    Innovative Condition of Probation." Journal of Criminal
                    Law and Criminology 73: 604-61.

McKay, I.
    1987   "Springhill 1958." in G. Burrill and I. McKay (eds.), People,
                    Resources, and Power. Halifax: Gorsebrook Research
                    Institute.

McMullan, J., and P. Swan
    1989   "Social Economy and Arson in Nova Scotia." Canadian
                    Journal of Criminology 31: 281-308.

Merchant, C.
    1980   The Death of Nature: Women, Ecology and the Scientific
                    Revolution. London: Wildwood House.

Merton, R.K.
    1957   Social Theory and Social Structure. New York: Free Press.

Michalos, A.
1980   *Crime, Justice and Politics.* Volume 2 of North American Social Report, *A Comparative Study of the Quality of Life* in Canada and the U.S.A. from 1964 to 1974. Boston: D. Reidel Co.

Michalowski, R.
1985   Order, Law and Crime: An Introduction to Criminology. New York: Random House.

Michalowski, R. and R.C. Kramer
1987   "The Space Between Laws: the Problem of Corporate Crime in a Transnational Context." Social Problems 34, no. 1: 34-53.

Michaud, L.
1988   "A Travesty of Justice: How One Man's Hell Became a Concern for All." At the Source 9, no. 1: 4-6.

Miller, A.S.
1973   "Courts and Corporate Accountability." In R. Nader and M. Green (eds.), Corporate Power in America. New York: Grossman.

Mintz, M.
1985   At Any Cost: Corporate Greed, Women and the Dalkon Shield. New York: Pantheon.

Mintz, M.
1987   "At Any Cost: Corporate Greed, Women and the Dalkon Shield." In Stuart Hills (ed.), Corporate Violence, Injury and Death for Profit. Tatowa, N.J.: Rowman and Littlefield.

Monahan, J., and Novaco, R.
1979   "Corporate Violence: A Psychological Analysis." In A. Lipsett and B. Sales (eds.), New Directions in Psychological Research. New York: Van Nostrand.

Nader, R.
1970   "The Profits of Pollution." The Progressive 34 (April).

Nader, R., and M. Green, eds.
1973   Corporate Power in America. New York: Grossman.

Nader, R., M.T. Green, and J. Seligman
1976   Taming the Giant Corporation. New York: Morton.

Offe, C.
1984   Contradictions of the Welfare State. London: Hutchison.

O'Malley, P.
1987   "Marxist Theory and Marxist Criminology." In Crime and Social Justice, no. 29: 70-87.

O'Neill, B.
    1987   "The Sinking of the Ocean Ranger, 1982: The Politics of a
                Resource Tragedy." In Gary Burrill and Ian McKay (eds.),
                People, Resources, and Power. Halifax: Gorsebrook
                Research Institute.

Orland, L.
    1980   "Reflections on Corporate Crime: Law in Search of Theory
                and Scholarship." American Criminal Law Review 17.

Parenti, M.
    1980   Democracy for the Few. New York: St. Martins Press.

Paulus, I.
    1974   The Search for Pure Food: A Sociology of Legislation in
                Britain. London: Martin Robertson.

Pearce, F.
    1973   "Crime, Corporations, and the American Social Order." In
                Ian Taylor and L. Taylor (eds.), Politics and Deviance.
                Baltimore: Penguin.

Pearce, F.
    1978   Crimes of the Powerful. London: Pluto Press.

Pearce, F., and S. Tombs
    1989   "Bhopal: Union Carbide and the Hubris of Capitalist
                Technology." Social Justice 16, no. 2: 116-45.

Pearce, F., and S. Tombs
    1990   "Ideology, Hegemony and Empiricism Compliance Theories
                of Regulation." *British Journal of Criminology* 30: 4.

Peltzman, J.
    1976   "Toward a More General Theory of Regulation." Journal of
                Law and Economics 19: 211-40.

Perrow, C.
    1961   "The Analysis of Goals in Complex Organizations."
                American Sociological Review 26 (December): 854-65.

Perrow, C.
    1970   *Organizational Analysis: A* Sociological View. Belmont:
                Brooks/Cole.

Perrow, C.
    1972   Complex Organizations: A Critical Essay. Chicago: Scott,
                Foresman.

Perry, S., and Dawson, J.
    1985   Nightmare: Women and the Dalkon Shield. New York:
                MacMillan.

Pringle, R.
1989   "Bureaucracy, Rationality and Sexuality: The Case of
              Secretaries." In J. Hearn, D.L. Sheppard, P. Tancred-Sherriff
              and G. Burrel (eds.), *The Sexuality of Organization*. London:
              Sage.

Rakoff, J.
1985   "The Exercise of Prosecutorial Discretion in Federal
              Business Fraud Prosecutions." In B. Fisse and French (eds.),
              Corrigible Corporations and Unruly Law. San Antonio:
              Trinity University Press.

Rankin, R., and R. Brown
1985   "The Treatment of Repeat Offenders under B.C.'s
              Occupational Health and Safety and Pollution Control
              Legislation." Paper presented at the Canadian Law and
              Society Association, Windsor, June.

Ratner, R.S., J.L. McMullan and B. Burtch
1987   "The Problem of Relative Autonomy and Criminal Justice in
              the Canadian State." In R. S. Ratner and J. L. McMullan
              (eds.), Criminal Justice Politics in Canada. University of
              British Columbia Press, Vancouver.

Reasons, C.E., L. Ross and C. Paterson
1981   Assault on the Worker: Occupational Health and Safety in
              Canada. Toronto: Butterworths.

Reasons, C.E.
1982   "Crime and the Abuses of Power: offences and offenders
              beyond the reach of the law." In P. Wickman and T. Dailey
              (eds.), White Collar and Economic Crime. Lexington, Mass.:
              D. C. Heath.

Reasons, C.E., ed.
1984   Calgary Ltd: An Untold Story. Toronto: Between the Lines.

Reasons, C.E.
1987   "Workplace Terrorism." The Facts 9, no. 3: 6-11.

Reiman, J.
1979   The Rich Get Richer and the Poor Get Prison. New York:
              John Wiley.

Richardson, B.
1989   "The Lubicon of Northern Alberta Wrestling with the
              Canadian System: A Decade of Lubicon Frustration." In B.
              Richardson (ed.), Drumbeat Anger and Renewal in Indian
              Country. Toronto: Summerhill.

Ross, E.A.
1907   Sin and Society: An Analysis of Latter-Day Inequity. New
              York: Harper and Row.

Sargent, N.
    1989   "Law, Ideology and Corporate Crime: A Critique of
                   Instrumentalism." Canadian Journal of Law and Society,
                   no. 4: 39-75.

Sargent, N.
    1990   Law, Ideology and Social Change: An Analysis of the Role
                   of Law in the Construction of Corporate Crime." Journal of
                   Human Justice 1, no. 2: 97-116.

Schlegel, K.
    1988   "Desert, Retribution, and Corporate Criminology." Justice
                   Quarterly 5, no. 4: 615-34.

Scholz, J.
    1984   "Voluntary Compliance and Regulatory Enforcement."
                   Law and Policy 6: 385-404.

Schrager, L.S. and J.F. Short
    1978   "Toward a Sociology of Organizational Crime." Social
                   Problems 25, no. 4: 407-19.

Schrager, L.S. and J.F. Short
    1980   "How serious a crime? Perceptions of organizational and
                   common crimes." In G. Geis and E. Stotland (eds.), White
                   Collar Crime: Theory and Research. New York: Sage.

Schrecker, T.F.
    1984   The Political Economy of Environmental Hazards. Ottawa:
                   Minister of Supply and Services.

Schrecker, T.F.
    1989   "The Political Context and Content of Environmental Law."
                   In T. Caputo et al. (eds.), Law and Society: A Critical
                   Perspective. Toronto: Harcourt Brace Jovanovich.

Schwendinger, H., and J. Schwendinger
    1970   "Defenders of Order or Guardian of Human Rights." Issues
                   in Criminology 5, no. 2.

Scott, D.W.
    1989   "Policing Corporate Collusion." Criminology 27, no. 3: 559-
                   87.

Segal, L.
    1987   Is the Future Female? Troubled Thoughts on Contemporary
                   Feminism. London: Virago Press.

Segal, L.
    1990   Slow Motion: Changing Masculinities Changing Men.
                   London: Virago Press.

Shapiro, S.P.
1984   Wayward Capitalists Target of the Securities and Exchange
            Commission. New Haven: Yale University Press.

Shapiro, S.P.
1985   "The Road Not Taken: The Elusive Path to Criminal
            Prosecution for White Collar Offenders." Law and Society
            Review 19, no. 2.

Sheppard, D.L.
1989   "Organizations, Power and Sexuality: The Image and Self-
            Image of Women Managers." In J. Hearn, D.L. Sheppard, P.
            Tancred-Sherriff and G. Burrel (eds.), *The Sexuality of
            Organization*. London: Sage.

Sherrill, R.
1987   "Murder Inc: What Happens to Corporate Criminals?" Utne
            Reader (March/April).

Shkilnyk, A.
1985   A Poison Stronger Than Love. The Destruction of an Ojibwa
            Community. New Haven: Yale University.

Shover, N.
1980   "The Criminalization of Corporate Behaviour: Federal
            Surface Coal Mining." In G. Geis and E. Stotland (eds.),
            White Collar Crime: Theory and Research. Beverly Hills:
            Sage.

Silk, L. and D. Vogel
1976   Ethics and Profits: The Crisis of Confidence in American
            Business. New York: Simon and Schuster.

Simon, D.R., and D. S. Eitzen
1986   Elite Deviance. Newton: Allyn and Bacon.

Sinden, P.G.
1980   "Perceptions of Crime in Capitalist America: The Question
            of Consciousness Manipulation." Sociological Focus 13: 75-
            85.

Smandych, R.
1985   "Marxism and the Creation of Law Re-Examining the
            Origins of Canadian Anti-combines Legislation, 1890-1910."
            In Thomas Fleming (ed.), The New Criminologies in
            Canada: State, Crime and Control. Toronto: Oxford
            University Press.

Smart, C.
1989   *Feminism and the Power of Law*. London: Routledge.

Snider, L.
  1978   "Corporate Crime in Canada: A Preliminary Report."
               Canadian Journal of Criminology 20, no. 2: 142-68.

Snider, L.
  1979   "Revising the Combines Investigation Act: A Study of
               Corporate Power." In P. Brantingham and J. Kress (eds.),
               Structure, Law and Power. Beverley Hills: Sage

Snider, L., and G. West
  1980   "A Critical Perspective on Law in the Canadian State:
               Delinquency and Corporate Crime." In Richard Ossenberg
               (ed.), Power and Change in Canada. Toronto: McClelland
               and Stewart.

Snider, L.
  1982   "Traditional and Corporate Theft: A Comparison of
               Sanctions." In P. Wickman and T. Dailey (eds.), White Collar
               and Economic Crime Toronto: Lexington Books.

Snider, L.
  1987   "Towards a Political Economy of Reform, Regulation and
               Corporate Crime." Law and Policy 9, no. 1: 37-68.

Snider, L.
  1988   "Commercial Crime." In Vincent F. Sacco (ed.), Deviance
               Conformity and Control in Canadian Society. Scarborough:
               Prentice-Hall.

Snider, L.
  1990   "Cooperative Models to Control Corporate Crime: Panacea
               or Cop Out?" Unpublished paper.

Snider, L.
  1991   "The Regulatory Dance: Understanding Reform Processes in
               Corporate Crime", International Journal of the Sociology of
               Law, 19:237-272.

Staffman, D.
  1984   "Fear and Loathing: the sad tale of how the asbestos
               industry went very, very wrong." Canadian Business 57,
               no. 15: 15-18.

Stanley, D.T., D.E. Mann and J.W. Doig
  1967   Men Who Govern. Washington: Brookings Institute.

Stigler, G.
  1975   The Citizen and the State: Essays on Regulation. Chicago:
               University of Chicago Press.

Stone, C.
1975   Where the Law Ends: The Social Control of Corporate Behavior. New York: Harper & Row.

Stone, C.
1978   "Social Control of Corporate Behavior." In D. Ermann and R. Lundman (eds.), Corporate and Government Deviance: *Problems of Organization in Contemporary Society.* New York: Oxford University Press.

Sumner, C.
1981   "The Rule of Law and Civil Rights in Contemporary Marxist Theory." Kapitalstate 9: 63-90.

Supreme Court of Canada
1989   *Irwin Toy Ltd.* v. *Quebec (Attorney General).* Reports. Ottawa: Supreme Court.

Sutherland, E.
1961   White Collar Crime. New York: Holt, Rinehart and Winston.

Sutherland, E.
1973   "Crime of Corporations." In Karl Schuessler (ed.), On Analyzing Crime. Chicago: University of Chicago Press.

Swartz, J.
1978   "Silent Killers at Work." In M.D. Ermann and R. J. Lundman (eds.), Corporate and Governmental Deviance: Problems of Organization in Contemporary Society. New York: Oxford University Press.

Swimmer, G., and S. Luce
1985   "Asbestos Exposure and Attitudes Toward Occupational Health." Relations Industrielles 40, no. 3: 529-44.

Szasz, A.
1986   "Corporations, organized crime, and the disposal of hazardous waste: An examination of the making of a criminogenic regulatory structure." Criminology 24: 1-27.

Tallmer, M.
1987   "Chemical Dumping as a Corporate Way of Life." In Stuart Hills (ed. Corporate Violence, Injury and Death for Profit. Tatowa, N.J.: Rowman and Littlefield.

Thomas, J.
1982   "The Regulatory Role in the Containment of Corporate Illegality." In Herbert Edelhertz and Thomas Overcast (eds.), White Collar Crime: An Agenda for Research. Toronto: Lexington Books.

Thompson, E.P.
   1977   Whigs and Hunters: The Origins of the Black Act.
                 Harmondsworth, U.K.: Perigrine Books.

Thompson, E.P.
   1980   Writing by Candlelight. London, Merlin Books.

Time
   1985   "Environmental Harm." October 14.

Tolson, A.
   1977   The Limits of Masculinity. London: Tavistock.

Tudivier, S.
   1986   "The strength of links: International women's health
                 networks in the eighties." In K. McDonnell (ed.), Adverse
                 Effects: Women and the Pharmaceutical Industry. Toronto:
                 Women's Press.

Turner, B.
   1986   Citizenship and Capitalism: The Debate Over Reformism.
                 London: Allen and Unwin.

Vandivier, K.
   1978   "Why Should My Conscience Bother Me?" In M. David
                 Ermann and Richard J. Lundman (eds.), Corporate and
                 Government Deviance. New York: Oxford University Press.

Vaughan, D.
   1979   "Crime Between Organizations: Implications for
                 Victimology." In Gilbert Geis and Ezra Stotland (eds.),
                 White Collar Crime. Beverly Hills, Calif.: Sage.

Vaughan, D.
   1983   Controlling Unlawful Organizational Behavior: Social
                 Structure and Corporate Misconduct. Chicago: University of
                 Chicago Press.

Veltmeyer, H.
   1987   Canadian Corporate Power. Toronto: Garamond Press.

Vogel, D.
   1986   National Styles of Regulation: Environmental Policy in
                 Great Britain and the United States. Ithaca, N.Y.: Cornell
                 University Press.

Von Hirsch, A.
   1985   Past or Future Crimes: Deservedness and Dangerousness in
                 the Sentencing of Criminals. New Brunswick, N.J.: Rutgers
                 University Press.

Waldram, J.B.
1988   As Long as the River Runs: Hydroelectric Development and
              Native Communities in Western Canada. Winnipeg:
              University of Manitoba.

Walters, V.
1985   "The Politics of occupational health and safety: interviews
              with workers' health and safety representatives and
              company doctors." Canadian Review of Sociology and
              Anthropology 22, no. 2: 57-79.

Ward, T.
1986   "Symbols and Noble Lies, Abolitionism 'Just Deserts' and
              Crimes of the Powerful." In H. Bianchi and R. Van
              Swaaningen (eds.), Abolitionism: Towards a Non-
              Repressive Approach to Crime. Amsterdam: Free University
              Press.

Waters, J.A.
1978   "Catch22: Corporate Morality as an Organizational
              Phenomenon." Organizational Dynamics 20, no. 5 (spring).

Weber, M.
1978   Economy and Society. Volume 1. Los Angeles: University of
              California Press.

Wente, M.
1984   "The coming crisis in workers compensation." Canadian
              Business 57, no. 14: 46-50.

Wheeler, S., and M. Rothman
1982   "The Organization as Weapon in White Collar Crime."
              Michigan Law Review 80, no. 7: 1403-26.

Winter, G.
1985   "Bartering Rationality in Regulation." Law and Society
              Review 19, no. 2: 219-50.

Wright, J. P.
1979   On a Clear Day You Can See General Motors: John
              DeLorean's Look Inside the Automotive Giant. New York:
              Avon.

Yoder, S.
1978   "Criminal Sanctions for Corporate Illegality." Journal of
              Criminal Law and Criminology 69: 40-58.

Young, B.
1974   "Corporate Interests and the State." Our Generation 10, no.
              1: 70-79.